INFORMATION AND COMMUNICATION TECHNOLOGIES IN EVERYDAY LIFE: OPPORTUNITIES AND CHALLENGES

Information and Communication Technologies in Everyday Life: Opportunities and Challenges

Prof. Al-Dahoud Ali

Contributors

Mustafa Ibrahim
Mohamed Waleed Fakhr
Mustafa Abdel Aziem
Giorgi Gabunia
Chantal Cherifi
Muhammed Yousoof
Mohd Sapiyan
Sonja Ristić.
Slavica Aleksić.
Milan Čeliković.
Ivan Luković.
Udo Richard Averweg

 **UbiCC Research Publishing**
2014

Contribution Acknowledgement

I would like to acknowledge the contribution of all the fellows, without their support it would have been difficult to complete this project. Following are the name of the authors along with their contributed chapters.

- **Chapter 1**

  Mustafa Ibrahim   *The Arab Academy for Science, Technology and Maritime Transport, Egypt*
  Mohamed Waleed Fakhr   *The Arab Academy for Science, Technology and Maritime Transport, Egypt*
  Mustafa Abdel Aziem   *The Arab Academy for Science, Technology and Maritime Transport, Egypt*

- **Chapter 2**

  Chantal Cherifi   *University of Lyon2, France*

- **Chapter 3**

  Muhammed Yousoof   *Dhofar University*
  Mohd Sapiyan   *Gulf University of Science and Technology*

- **Chapter 4**

  Sonja Ristić.   *University of Novi Sad*
  Slavica Aleksić.   *University of Novi Sad*
  Milan Čeliković.   *University of Novi Sad*
  Ivan Luković.   *University of Novi Sad*

- **Chapter 5**

  Udo Richard Averweg   *eThekwini Municipality and University of KwaZulu-Natal, South Africa*

First Printing: 2014

ISBN 978-1-312-55980-6

UbiCC Research Publishing
www.ubicc.org
info@ubicc.org

Dedication

To all Humanity

Contents

Foreword

It is with great honor that I write this Foreword for the book Information and Communication Technologies in Everyday Life: Opportunities and Challenges. Information and communication technology has become one of the basic building blocks of modern society and has seamlessly integrated with people everyday life. Dr. Al-Dahuod who is well known researcher in the domain has put a tremendous effort by putting together the best work presented by experts in the domain. The contributions presented in this book are selected from different continents of the world, which gives an idea about how the technology has evolved in peoples' life across different continents. The topic presented in the book is very interesting and of great importance in the research domain. I am convinced that the present publication will furnish to scientific groups, young researchers, industry and new graduate student as an excellent reference book. Every chapter of the book presents a discussion along the state of art and expresses a perfect connection with the following chapter, which can help research working in different fields to work on common interest areas. It gives me pleasure to recognize the true international co-operation of research to present such a wonderful work, and lastly, I would wish to recognize the efforts of Dr. Al-Dahuod who organized this cooperation to present the collective contribution.

David James (Ph.D.)
Editor-in-Chief
UbiCC Journal

Preface

The idea behind this book emerges from the accumulative experience of conference organization. Since I organized many conferences as General or Program Chair, it, gives me an opportunity to meet young researchers and graduate students and participate in the discussion over brainstorming session and dinners, to get to know their challenges and difficulties in pursuing research in a specific domain for their study in information engineering. I attempted in this book to invite contribution from the best researchers around the globe and accumulate them in single topographic point and assist young researchers to look up this book while perusing their research topic. I hope this book will serve as a reference book for young researchers in Information communication domain and other peers to compare their results.

Introduction

This book consists of five chapters that cover many aspects in Information Technology. The chapters are organized as follows:

- Chapter 1: This chapter presents discussion about large scale linear coding for image classification. Image classification, including object recognition and scene classification, remains to be a major challenge to the computer vision community. As machine can be able to extract information from an image and classify it in order to solve some tasks. Recently SVMs using Spatial Pyramid Matching (SPM) kernel have been highly successful in image classification. Despite its popularity, this technique cannot handle more than thousands of training images. In this chapter, author develop an extension of the SPM method, by generalizing Vector Quantization to Sparse Coding followed by multi-scale Spatial Max Pooling, and also propose a large scale linear classifier based on Scale Invariant Feature Transform (SIFT) and Sparse Codes. This new adapted algorithm remarkably can handle thousands of training images and classify them into different categories.

- Chapter 2: This chapter presents discussion about the enhancing web services classification using similarity networks. The diversity of users' needs and the ever growing number of Web services makes the discovering of the appropriate ones a challenging issue. In order to enhance the composition life cycle, an efficient organization of the Web services landscape must be integrated within discovery and substitution mechanisms. Classically, Web services are organized into non-overlapping categories based on a similarity metric. The main drawback of this approach is that it lacks the precise information that is needed toward Web service selection within a category. In this paper, we propose a finer organization based on networks. The nodes of the networks are the operations of the Web services while the links join similar operations. Four similarity measures based on the comparison of input and output parameters values of Web services operations are presented. A comparative evaluation of the topological structure of the corresponding networks is performed on a benchmark of semantically annotated Web services. Results show that, with this approach, we get a deeper and more subtle vision of the functional similarities between Web services.

- Chapter 3: this chapter presents discussion about the measuring cognitive load for visualizations in learning computer programming -physiological measures. Computer programming is a complex skill to acquire for novice learners who are in their initial phase of learning programming. There are many factors that results in difficulties in learning programming. This paper addresses to resolve one core difficulty which is cognitive load [2] [3].Cognitive load theory [13] is a famous theory of learning. It states that the schema of the long term memory is not well built in the case of novices and also there is a limitation of working memory's capacity. This makes it hard for novices to understand the concepts and equip with the skills necessary to become programmers. Some efforts used to overcome the cognitive load are the visualization tools for learning programming [14] .There is no accountability on how effective these visualization systems helped in reducing the load. The mechanism to measure cognitive load is not used in the visualization systems. There are two methods of cognitive load measurement namely physiological and non-physiological measures. Physiological measures include EKG, GSR [12], EEG [11], Temperature [11] etc. and non-physiological measures includes rating scale [6] and some recent research studies have used EEG as an index for cognitive load measurement [7]. We felt that using the physiological measures could be accurate as they are the reflections of the body impulses. There is no user's control over the measurement. We also decided to use EEG as the latest efforts of measuring the cognitive uses EEG. The study also employed one more physiological measure namely GSR. This paper addresses the cognitive load measurement while using visualization tools by the novice programmers using EEG and GSR as an index of cognitive load.

- Chapter 4: This chapter presents discussion about the meta-models in support of database model transformations. Model-Driven Software Engineering (MDSE) aims to provide automated support for the development, maintenance and evolution of software by performing transformations on models. During these transformations model elements are traced from a more abstract model to a more concrete model and vice versa, achieved through meta-modeling. Software development process produces numerous models of complex application artifacts, such as application programs, databases, web sites or user interfaces (UI). In the paper we focus on models related to databases. For these models we use a generic name database models. They may be created at several, usually different levels of abstraction. In order to specify and generate model transformations between these database models, theirs meta-models have to be defined. In the paper, we propose a classification of database models and meta-models that are involved in the database model transformations. Also, we present a meta-model of relational database schema specified by means of the Eclipse Modeling Framework (EMF) and based on the EMF Ecore meta-model which is closely aligned with the Essential MOF (EMOF) specification.

- Chapter 5: This chapter presents discussion about the two study findings in South Africa of the technology acceptance model: a comparative analysis. Models for information technology (IT) adoption build on theories of behavioral change and attempt to better understand what motivates and influences the adoption of technologies. One popular technology is an Executive Information System (EIS). An EIS is a computerized information system, designed to provide managers in organizations with access to internal and external information that is relevant to management activities and decision-making. IT acceptance studies pay much attention to issues of significance in assessing the contributions of variables explaining IT usage for decision-making in organizations. Davis' Technology Acceptance Model (TAM) states that Perceived Usefulness (PU) and Perceived Ease of Use

(PEOU) are the two factors that govern the adoption and use of IT. In this article, discussion is made of the findings of two TAM/EIS studies in the eThekwini Municipal Area (EMA), KwaZulu-Natal, South Africa. From these TAM/EIS studies, are four findings: (1) low correlation coefficients were calculated for the PU-AT and PEOU-AT constructs; (2) the correlation for perceived usefulness-use was lower than for perceived ease of use-use, which is not consistent with Davis' findings; (3) the results partially support Venkatesh's findings [40] that PEOU can be a stronger catalyst (over PU) in fostering IT acceptance; and (4) there is support for Brown's findings [12] - wherein the TAM PEOU-AT relationship was higher than PU-AT.

Chapter 1

Large Scale Linear Coding For Image Classification

1. Introduction

One of the most significant developments in the last decade is the application of local features to image classification, including the introduction of "Bag-of-Words" (BoW) representation that inspires and initiates many research efforts [1]. In recent years, the Bag-of-Features (BoF) model has been extremely popular in image categorization [2]. The method treats an image as a collection of unordered appearance descriptors extracted from local patches, quantizes them into discrete "visual words", and then computes a compact histogram representation for semantic image classification, e.g. object recognition or scene categorization [2]. One particular extension of the BoF model, called Spatial Pyramid Matching (SPM) [3], has made a remarkable success on a range of image classification benchmarks like Caltech-101 [4] and Caltech-256 [2, 5].

Linear classification has become one of the most promising learning techniques for large sparse data with a huge number of instances and features. For example, it takes only several seconds to train an image classification problem from Caltech 101 that has more than 100,000 examples. For the same task, a traditional SVM solver such as LIBSVM would take several hours. Moreover, LIBLINEAR is even faster than state of the art linear classifiers such LIBSVM [6].

2. Problem Statement

The traditional SPM approach based on Bag-of-Features (BoF) requires nonlinear classifiers to achieve good image classification performance [7]. However, these results are not effective in classifying real data so using sparse coding with SPM allow us to use linear classifier instead of nonlinear, which used before, but the linear classifier still has limitation in huge data. There for, in this paper we proposed a technique that uses the capabilities of large-scale linear classifier in classification process with sparse coding spatial pyramid matching technique, which require a linear classifier to have good results with huge data.

3. Related Work

In computer vision, the Bag-of-Words model (BoW model) can be applied to image classification as Bag-of-Features model (BoF model), by treating image features as words. In document classification, a Bag of Words is a sparse vector of occurrence counts of words; that is, a sparse histogram over the vocabulary. In computer vision, a bag of visual words is a sparse vector of occurrence counts of vocabulary of local image features. To represent an image using BoW model, the image can be treated as a document. Similarly, "words" in images needs to be defined too. To achieve this, it usually passes by next three steps: Feature detection (computer vision), feature description and codebook generation [8]. A definition of the BoW model can be the "histogram representation based on independent features" [9].

The BoF approach discards the spatial order of local descriptors, which severely limits the descriptive power of the image representation. By overcoming this problem, one particular extension of the BoF model, called Spatial Pyramid Matching (SPM) [3] had made a remarkable success on a range of image classification benchmarks like Caltech-101 [4] and Caltech-256 [2, 5].

Researchers have found that [2], in order to obtain good performances, both BoF and SPM must be applied together with a particular type of nonlinear Mercer kernels, e.g. the intersection kernel or the Chi-square kernel. Accordingly, we can say that, the traditional SPM approach based on (BoF) requires nonlinear classifiers to achieve good image classification performance [7]. The nonlinear SVM method using SPM kernels [10,11] seems to be dominant among the top performers in various image classification benchmarks, the nonlinear SVM has to pay a computational complexity $O(n3)$ and a memory complexity $O(n2)$ in the training phase, where n is the training size. Furthermore, since the number of support vectors grows linearly with n, the computational complexity in testing is $O(n)$. This scalability implies a severe limitation as it is nontrivial to apply them to real-world applications, whose training size is typically far beyond thousands [2].

Using Sparse coding with spatial pyramid matching can to represent each image by single image feature where the output of SIFT algorithm (local feature vectors for each image) becomes the input to coding phase ScSPM as shown in figure. 1 sample. By using this technique, we overcome on the need to use nonlinear classifier in the level of classification.

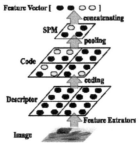

Figure 1. Spatial pyramid structure for pooling features for image classification [7].

4. Encoding Features from Vector Unitization to Sparse Coding

Let X be a set of SIFT appearance descriptors in a D-dimensional feature space, i.e. $X= [x1. . . xM] T \in \mathbb{R} M x D$. The Vector Quantization (VQ) method applies the K-means clustering algorithm to solve the following problem [2].

$$\min_{V} \sum_{m=1}^{M} \min_{k=1...k} \| x_m - v_k \|^2 \quad (1)$$

Where V= [v1. . . vk] T are the K cluster centers to be found, called codebook, and ‖ . ‖ denotes the L2-norm of vectors [2]. The optimization problem can be reformulated into a matrix factorization problem with cluster membership indicators

$$\min_{U,V} \sum_{m=1}^{M} \| x_m - u_m V \|^2 \quad (2)$$

Subject to Card $(u_m) = 1, | u_m| = 1, u_m \geq 0, \forall m$

Where Card $(u_m) = 1$ is a cardinality constraint, meaning that only one element of u_m is nonzero, $u_m \geq 0$ means that all the elements of u_m are nonnegative, and $| u_m|$ is the L1-norm of u_m, the summation of the absolute value of each element in u_m. After the optimization, the index of the only nonzero element in u_m indicates which cluster the vector x_m belongs to. In the training phase of VQ, the optimization Eq. (2) is solved with respect to both U and V. In the coding phase, a learned V which will be applied to a new set of Then Eq. (2) solved with respect to U only [2].

The constraint Card $(u_m) = 1$ may be too restrictive, giving rise to often a coarse reconstruction of X. to relax the constraint by instead putting L1-norm regularization on u_m, which enforces u_m to have a small number of nonzero elements. Then the VQ formulation turned into another problem known as sparse coding (SC):

$$\min_{U,V} \sum_{m=1}^{M} \| x_m - u_m V \|^2 + \lambda |u_m| \quad (3)$$

Subject to $\| v_k \| \leq 1, \quad \forall k = 1,2,....K$

Where a unit L2-norm constraint on vk typically applied to avoid trivial Eq. (1) [2]. Normally, the codebook V is an over complete basis set, i.e. K > D-dimensional. Note that we drop out the no negativity constraint $u_m \geq 0$ as well, because the sign of u_m is not essential, it can be easily absorbed by letting $T \leftarrow = [VT, - VT]$ and $u_m^T \leftarrow [u_{m+}^T, -u_{m-}^T]$ so that the constraint can be trivially satisfied, where $u_{m+}^T = \min(0, u_m)$ and $u_{m-}^T = \max(0, u_m)$.

Similar to VQ, SC has a training phase and a coding phase. First, a descriptor set X from a random collection of image patches is used to solve Eq. (3) with respect to U and V, where V is retained as the codebook. In the coding phase, for each image represented as a descriptor set X, the SC codes are obtained by optimizing Eq. (3) with respect to U only [2].

Sparse Coding has been chosen to derive image representations because it has a number of attractive properties. First, compared with the VQ coding, SC coding can achieve a much lower reconstruction error due to the less restrictive constraint, second, sparsely allows the representation to be specialized, and to capture salient properties of images, third, research in image statistics clearly reveals that image patches are sparse signals [2].

5. Linear Spatial Pyramid Matching

For any image represented by a set of descriptors, a single feature vector based on some statistics of the descriptors' codes can be computed. For example, if U is obtained via Eq. (2), a popular choice is to compute the histogram

$$z = \frac{1}{M} \sum_{m=1}^{M} u_m \qquad (4)$$

The Bag-of-Words approach to image classification computes such a histogram z for each image I represented by an unordered set of local descriptors. In the more sophisticated SPM approach, the image's Spatial Pyramid histogram representation z is a concatenation of local histograms in various partitions of different scales. After normalization, z can be seen as again a histogram. Let zi denote the histogram representation for image Ii [2]. For a binary image classification problem, an SVM aims to learn a decision function

$$f(z) = \sum_{i=1}^{n} \alpha_i \, k(z, z_i) + b \qquad (5)$$

Where f $\{(zi; yi)\}$ n i=1 is the training set, and yi∈ {-1; +1} indicates labels. For a test image represented by z, if f (z) > 0 then the image is classified as positive, otherwise as negative [2].

6. Large Scale Linear Coding For Image Classification

This paper follows another line of research on building discriminative models for classification. The previous work includes nonlinear SVMs using pyramid matching kernels [10] and K-Nearest Neighbor (KNN) methods [11, 12, 13], or Linear ScSPM technique as shown in Figure. 2, Over the past years experimental results, have shown that Linear Sparse coding Spatial Pyramid Matching "Linear ScSPM" not enough for real-world application contain thousands of images. Where this technique was tried to use it to classify 2000 image (100 category each one has 10 images for training and 10 images for testing) but it cannot do that as shown in Table (1) using Intel Core 2 Duo 2.33 GHz and 4 GB RAM Dell machine.

Therefore, this technique tried to employ the powerful of the previous technique "linear ScSPM" and in the same time, it handles the limitation of classifying thousands of real word data. Large scale linear classifier "liblinear-1.91" could to handle these limitations perfectly Figure. 2.

Using Scale Invariant Feature Transform (SIFT) algorithm local feature descriptors for each image can be extracted then Sparse coding with Spatial Pyramid Matching (ScSPM) encode the extracted features into single features vector which represent the salient properties of images Figure.3, whereupon, Large scale linear classifier can be used to classify large scale of data speedily and accurately.

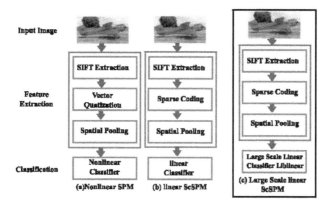

Figure 2 (a) Traditional way using nonlinear classifier **(b)** linear classifier with sparse coding spatial pyramid matching **(c)** large scale linear classifier [2].

Table 1 Limitation of Linear SCSPM in Classifying Data

Experiments	# categories	#Training data	#Testing data	Mean accuracy
1	2	20	20	100%
2	2	25	25	100%
3	5	25	25	93.28%
4	10	25	25	91.13%
5	15	25	25	82.53%
6	100	5	5	58.08%
7	100	10	10	Error out of Memory

Sparse coding measures the responses of each local descriptor to the dictionary's visual elements. These responses are pooled across different spatial locations over different spatial scales. Linear classification has become one of the most promising learning techniques for large sparse data with a huge number of instances and features. Using linear- SVM "LIBLINEAR" instead of traditional SVM "LIBSVM" thousands of images can be classified perfectly, where, LIBLINEAR is optimized to deal with linear classification (i.e. no kernels necessary), whereas linear classification is only one of the many capabilities of libsvm, So logically it may not match up to LIBLINEAR in terms of classification accuracy [6].

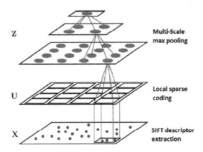

Figure 3 The Architecture of New Algorithm Based On Sparse Coding [2].

LIBLINEAR supports two popular binary linear classifiers: LR and linear SVM. Given a set of instance-label pairs (xi; yi); i = 1.., l, xi   Rn, yi   {+1,-1}, both methods solve the Following unconstrained optimization problem with different loss functions ε(w; xi; yi)

$$\min_{w} \frac{1}{2}w^T w + C \sum_{i=1}^{l} \xi(w; x_i; y_i) \qquad (6)$$

Where, C > 0 is a penalty parameter. For SVM, the two common loss functions are max (1-yiwTxi; 0) and max (1-yiwTxi, 0)2. The former is referred to as L1-SVM, while the latter is L2-SVM. For LR, the loss function is log (1+e^{-} yiwTxi), which derived from a probabilistic model. The tool is available at [16].

7. Experiment and Results

By evaluating our technique on real data using IMAGENET and Caltech-101 dataset, hundreds of classes have been chosen to test our algorithm comparing with IMAGENET competition results September 16 2010, and libsvm experimental results 2011 [2].We represent results of Locality-constrained Linear Coding (LLC) algorithm that only used single descriptor (HoG) and simple linear SVM as the classifier. Using Caltech-256 dataset shown in figure. 4 [7]. In our experiments we only used one patch size to extract SIFT descriptors, namely, 16 x 16 pixels as in SPM [3], maximum image size was 300 x 300 pixels for width and height. In addition, we used LIBLINEAR -1.91 libraries as large-scale linear classifier using our algorithm, we conducted several experiments and here we represent some results of our experiments. In table 2 appear the results of classifying 25 categories, while in table 3 represents a comparison among our results and other techniques in ECCV2010 and PASCAL VOC 2009. Figure.5 represents some results of classifying 97categories using Caltech 101 dataset. Finally figure. 6 illustrate chart that represent the number of categories whose achieve specific ratio in classifying 97 categories using 3395 image "15 image in training and 20 image in testing" where x-axis represent ratio of success while y-axis represent number of categories achieved this ratio. We executed many experiments and compared their results with

ECCV2010 [1, 7], libsvm experimental results 2011 and IMAGENET results. Results demonstrated that our technique quickly reaches the testing accuracy

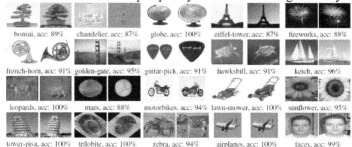

Figure 4: Example images from classes with highest classification accuracy from the Caltech-256 dataset Classifying 97 categories using "LLC algorithm"[7]

corresponding to the optimal solution of ScSPM Figure. 2 show the scalability limitation problem. Figure 4 Example images from classes with highest classification accuracy from the Caltech-256 dataset Classifying 97 categories using "LLC algorithm"[7].

Table 2 Classifying 25 categories using Liblinearclassifier. "Our algorithm"

Training and Testing 25 categories Together			
category name	Success	Total	Ratio %
Chairs	44	50	88
Watches	44	50	88
Sunflower	42	50	84
Butterflies	44	50	88
Odo meter	45	50	90
cap opener	35	50	70
Snowplow	39	50	78
Star anise	34	50	68
lunar craters	34	50	68
trolley bus	45	50	90
Geyser	48	50	96
Bonsi	38	50	76
Oak	5	50	10
China tree	10	50	20
teak Tect	13	50	26
Kentucky	25	50	50
airplanes	48	50	96
brain	49	50	98
car_side	50	50	100
chandelier	41	50	82
grand_piano	49	50	98
hawksbill	5	50	10
ketch	45	50	90
Leopards	46	50	92
Motorbikes	39	50	78
	917	1250	73.36

Table 3 Comparison of proposed method with top categories in ECCV 10. [1]

AP(%)	LEOBEN	LIP6	LEAR	FIRSTNIKON	CVC	UVASURREY SVC	linear SVMs	OURS
airplanes	79.5	80.9	79.5	83.3	86.3	84.7	87.1	**95**
bird	57.2	53.8	54.5	62.7	66.4	66.1	65.8	**90**
car	55.1	53.4	66.4	58.2	64.7	63.2	69.7	**100**
chair	51.1	50.7	54.4	54.3	55.5	57.1	58.5	**95**
motorbike	58.4	58	64.2	62.9	68.9	70.6	70.8	**90**
average	60.26	59.36	63.8	64.28	68.36	68.34	70.38	**94**

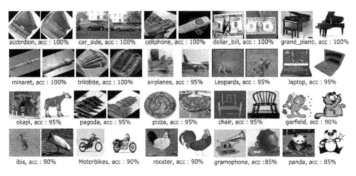

Figure 5 Example images from classes with highest classification accuracy from the Caltech-101 dataset Classifying 97 categories

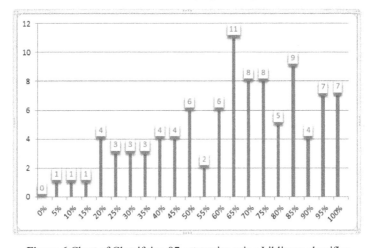

Figure 6 Chart of Classifying 97 categories using Liblinear classifier

8. Conclusion

In this paper we proposed a large-scale linear classifier liblinear using spatial pyramid matching approach based on SIFT sparse codes for image classification. The method uses selective Sparse Coding instead of traditional Vector Quantization to extract salient properties of appearance descriptors of local image patches. Furthermore, instead of averaging pooling in the histogram, sparse coding enables us to operate local max pooling on multiple spatial scales to incorporate translation and scale invariance. Where, each image can be encoded into single meaningful feature vector. The most encouraging result of this paper is the obtained image representation works surprisingly well with simple large-scale linear classifier liblinear, which dramatically improves the scalability of training and the speed of testing, and even improves the classification accuracy. Using 3395 image (97 categories), as a simple sample of large-scale data. Our experiments on a variety of image classification tasks demonstrated the effectiveness of this approach. As an indication from our work, the sparse codes of SIFT features might serve as a better local appearance descriptor for general image processing tasks.

9. Future Work

A recent work shows, that sparse coding approach can be accelerated by using a feed-forward network [14]. It will be interesting to try such methods to make our approach faster. Moreover, the accuracy could be improved by learning the codebook in a supervised fashion, as suggested by another recent work [15].

Summary

Image classification, including object recognition and scene classification, remains to be a major challenge to the computer vision community. As machine can be able to extract information from an image and classify it in order to solve some tasks. Recently SVMs using Spatial Pyramid Matching (SPM) kernel have been highly successful in image classification. Despite its popularity, this technique cannot handle more than thousands of training images. In this paper we develop an extension of the SPM method, by generalizing Vector Quantization to Sparse Coding followed by multi-scale Spatial Max Pooling, and also propose a large scale linear classifier based on Scale Invariant Feature Transform (SIFT) and Sparse Codes. This new adapted algorithm remarkably can handle thousands of training images and classify them into different categories.

References

1. Xi Zhouy, Kai Yuz, Tong Zhang, and Thomas S. Huangy, "Image Classification using Super-Vector Coding of Local Image Descriptors", Dept. of ECE, University of Illinois at Urbana-Champaign, Illinois,NEC Laboratories America, California ,Department of Statistics, Rutgers University, New Jersey ECCV10,2010.
2. Jianchao Yangy, Kai Yuz, YihongGongz, Thomas Huangy, "Linear Spatial Pyramid Matching Using Sparse Coding for Image Classification", Beckman Institute, University of Illinois at Urbana-Champaign ,NEC Laboratories America, Cupertino, CA 95014, USA CVPR09,2009.
3. S. Lazebnik, C. Schmid, and J. Ponce,"Beyond bags of features: Spatial pyramid matching for recognizing natural scene categories", CVPR, 2006.
4. F.F.Li, R. Fergus, and P. Perona, "Learning generative visual models from few training" examples: an incremental Bayesian approach tested on 101 object categories. In CVPRWorkshop on GenerativeModel Based Vision, 2004.
5. C.C.Chang and C.J. Lin. "LIBSVM: a library for support vector machines", 2001, Software available at: http://www.csie.ntu.edu.tw/~cjlin/libsvm.
6. RongEn Fan, Kai-Wei Chang, ChoJui Hsieh, Xiang Rui Wang and Chih-Jen Lin,"LIBLINEAR: A Library for Large Linear Classification", Department of Computer Science, National Taiwan University, Taipei 106, Taiwan July 14, 2012.

7. Jinjun Wang†, Jianchao Yang, Kai Yu, FengjunLv, Thomas Huang, and Yihong Gong ,"Locality constrained Linear Coding for Image Classification", Akiira Media System, Palo Alto, California ,Beckman Institute, University of Illinois at Urbana-Champaign ,NEC Laboratories America, Inc., Cupertino, California,CVPR'10,2010.

8. L. FeiFei and P. Perona, "A Bayesian Hierarchical Model for Learning Natural Scene Categories", Procof IEEE Computer Vision and Pattern Recognition, pp. 524–531, 2005.

9. L. FeiFei, R. Fergus, and A. Torralba,"Recognizing and Learning Object Categories", CVPR 07 short course,2007.

10. Lazebnik, S.Schmid, C. Ponce, "Bags of features, Spatial pyramid matching for recognizing natural scene categories", Citeseer, 2006.

11. Bosch, A.Zisserman, and A. Munoz, "Representing shape with a spatial pyramid kernel", Proceedings of the 6th ACM international conference on Image and video retrieval, ACM 2007.

12. Makadia, A.Pavlovic, and V. Kumar, "New baseline for image annotation", Proc. ECCV08, 2008.

13. Torralba, A.Fergus, and R.Weiss, "Small codes and large image databases for recognition", IEEE Conference on Computer Vision and Pattern Recognition. CVPR08, 2008.

14. K. Kavukcuoglu, M. Ranzato, and Y. LeCun.Fast, "sparse coding algorithms with applications to object recognition", Technical report, Computational and Biological Learning Lab, NYU, 2008.

15. J. Mairal, F. Bach, J. Ponce, G. Sapiro, and A. Zisserman, "Supervised dictionary learning", NIPS, 2009.

16. http://www.csie.ntu.edu.tw/~cjlin/liblinear.

Chapter 2

Enhancing Web Services Classification Using Similarity Networks

1. Introduction

Web services are web-based software applications designed to be published, discovered and invoked for remote use. Those modular applications can be programmatically loosely coupled through the Web to form more complex ones. Two of the most popular problems in Web services technology are discovery and composition. Discovery consists in locating the providers that advertise Web services that can satisfy a service request. Composition arises when several Web services are needed to fulfill a request. The basic architecture of WSDL, SOAP and UDDI is insufficient to realize truly automatic Web services discovery and composition. To overcome this drawback, semantic Web service descriptions such as WSDL-S, SAWSDL, OWL-S and WSMO have been proposed.

Despite all these efforts, Web services discovery and composition are still highly complex tasks. The complexity, in general, comes from different sources. The scale effect is one of them. It is related to the proliferation of Web services. Their volatile aspect is another source of complexity. Indeed, providers may change, relocate, or even remove them. This results in a Web services space that is an evolving structure of a great number of atomic Web services. Additionally, we observe functional redundancy among Web services that can be differentiated by their Quality of Service (QoS). This leads to multiple potential solutions for composition synthesis.

Knowledge of the similarity between Web services appeared of paramount importance. It is a key for optimizing discovery and composition processes. A great deal of work on service architecture and semantic Web has been devoted to address the problem of Web service discovery. Discovery deals with finding a set of services that corresponds to a predetermined user request. Once the composite Web service is synthetized, it is deployed. During the deployment, one or more constituents of the composite service may become unavailable. Hence, there arises a need to replace such components with other components while maintaining the overall functionality of the composite service.

To render discovery and substitution more efficient, Web services can be classified. Classification aims at organizing the Web services space according to different criteria. Classification is an advanced task within the composition life cycle. This topic has already triggered a large amount of research. In [1] and [2], Web services are grouped when they belong to the same application domain. In [3],

[4], [5], [6] and [7], Web services are classified according to their functional similarity. During discovery or substitution, the choice between Web services of the same domain or between similar ones is then delegated to humans or to machines.

The similarity notion can be addressed from different point of views ranging from basic functional properties to higher level issues such as the quality of service. In this paper, we concentrate on the functional properties of Web services. In order to state that a Web service is similar to another one, the Web services descriptions must be analyzed. Information on functional properties can be found in the textual description or in the service name. But the most probative and direct information is nested within the interfaces that contain operations name, and parameters name and type. In [4], Web services are organized into communities of substitutable services. Each community is associated with a specific functionality represented by an ontological concept. Functionality is materialized by a set of operations. Hence, Web services within a community meet the same need and are defined as functionally similar. In [5], similar Web services are grouped into clusters. Parameters and operations names are associated to an ontological concept, which is processed by a lexical similarity measure. In [7], two degrees of interface similarity called equivalent and replacing are defined. Equivalent Web services have the same number of operations and parameters, and parameters are of the same type. A replacing Web service has an additional functionality.

In order to improve the results of the discovery and substitution processes, it is important to increase the number of similar Web services by offering a large range of possibilities. Furthermore, classification may be improved by a more structured organization of the Web services within the communities. Our work follows this line. We propose a network model to represent sets of similar Web services operations. Operations are the nodes and a link account for a similarity relationship between two operations. The main contribution of this work is on the definition and analysis of similarity measures for the functional comparison among Web services. The proposed network model allows the automated identification of substitutable Web services. It differentiates with majority of works that are efficient in the domain-based discovery context, but not well suited for the substitution process.

2. Network Model

In this paper, we focus on the functional aspect of semantic Web services. We restrict the definition of a Web service to a set of operations with their input and output parameters. We use the following notations. A Web service is represented by a Greek letter. Each operation labeled by a digit contains a set of input parameters noted I, and a set of output parameters noted O. Each parameter is associated to an ontological concept represented by a letter. Figure. 1 represents a Web service α with two operations 1 and 2, input parameter ontological concepts $I1 = \{a, b\}$, $I2 = \{c\}$, and output parameter ontological concepts $O1 = \{d\}$, $O2 = \{e, f\}$. In the following, we use for short the word "parameter" rather than "parameter ontological concept" to describe the semantics associated to a parameter. The similarity network model is based on the similarity between operations. We consider operations rather than Web services as atomic entities for two reasons. First, operations are the entities that are ultimately invoked. Second, it allows getting a more detailed analysis of the similarities

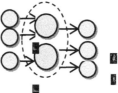

Figure 1 Schematic Representation of a Web Service

The similarity network model is based on the similarity between operations. We consider operations rather than Web services as atomic entities for two reasons. First, operations are the entities that are ultimately invoked. Second, it allows getting a more detailed analysis of the similarities. We define a similarity network as a graph whose nodes correspond to operations and links indicate a certain level of similarity between these operations. The nature of the similarity relationship is extremely important. It can be defined in several ways. We propose four operators that reflect different levels of functional similarity. These operators use a semantic matching function to compare the sets of input and output parameters. Thereafter, we describe the four similarity functions that we use to build the networks and we give their interpretation.

2.1. Similarity Functions

The four similarity functions are inspired by the work of [8] and [9] for service discovery. Several operators are presented and used to compare sets of ontological concepts in semantic descriptions. The definition of these operators is made on the key assumption that a user specifies his needs in terms of what he wants to achieve by using a service. In other words, the user knows the goals that he wants to get, but the way to reach them is not a major concern. To meet the needs, the request answer can be provided by an individual service or by a set of interacting services. The cornerstones elements are the goals pursued by the user, and they are represented by the output parameters of the Web service.

We selected four of these operators that reflect different matching situations between user's goals and the outputs provided by the services. We adapted these operator definitions to our goal, which is to determine a similarity value between two sets of parameters. The basic idea is that two Web services are substitutable if they allow reaching the same goal eventually using composite services.

FullSim is defined by analogy with the operator *Match*. It reflects the fact that all the user needs are met. *PartialSim* inspired by *Partial match* corresponds to the situation where only part of the goals is satisfied. Therefore, additional services will be needed to satisfy the request. The two other operators that we selected were introduced in [9] to take into account two situations ignored thus far. *ExcessSim* based on *Excess match* that expresses the case where the published service fully meets the goals of the user and provides more information. *RelationSim* is inspired from *Relation match* that has been introduced for situations where a service can meet the goals but the user cannot provide the inputs to invoke the service. To use such services, additional ones are required. The similarity functions (*FullSim, PartialSim, ExcessSim* and *RelationSim*) are defined in terms of set relations. Suppose we want to compare two operations i and j. I_i and I_j are respectively the sets of input parameters of i and j. O_i and O_j are respectively the sets of output parameters of i and j. We hence must compare I_i with I_j and O_i with O_j. *FullSim* means "full similarity". Two operations i and j are fully similar if they offer exactly the same set of output parameters ($O_i = O_j$) and if they have overlapping inputs ($I_i \cap I_j \neq \emptyset$). *PartialSim* means "partial similarity". Operation j is partially similar to operation i if some output parameters are missing in j ($O_i \supset O_j$) and if the two sets of input parameters overlap ($I_i \cap I_j \neq \emptyset$). *ExcessSim* means "excess similarity". An operation j is similar with excess to an operation i if j provides all the outputs of i plus additional ones ($O_i \subset O_j$) and if j has at most the inputs of ($I_i \supseteq I_j$). *RelationSim* means "relational similarity". Two operations i and j have a relational similarity if they have exactly the same outputs ($O_i = O_j$) and if they do not share any common input ($I_i \cap I_j = \emptyset$). FullSim and RelationSim are symmetric functions, while ExcessSim and PartialSim are asymmetric.

To achieve the comparison between individual parameters, we take as a basis the classical *exact* and *fail* subsumption relationships introduced in [10]. Let two parameters to be compared. In an *exact* matching, two parameters are similar if they are described by the same ontological concept. The *fail* matching means that there is no subsumption relation between the concepts associated to the parameters. Each similarity function allows building a specific network. In the following, we use the operators name to refer to the networks obtained with the different similarity functions. FullSim and RelationSim networks, due to the symmetrical nature of the similarity functions, are non-oriented networks. PartialSim and ExcessSim, which are derived from asymmetric functions, are oriented networks.

2.2. Interpretation of the Functions

To illustrate the different situations, we show through an example how the similarity functions can be interpreted. Let consider the six operations in Table 1. As stated previously, the user goal is the most important aspect to be considered. For example, suppose a user who wants to get the weather report of his city by providing the name and zip code of this city. Searching for operations that satisfy both the inputs and outputs can be too restrictive. Hence, we did not consider this case when designing the similarity functions. FullSim similarity can be considered as the second best solution, since it includes the expected outputs and some inputs of the request. Operations 4 and 5 are, in this case, two potential candidates. If no operation meets these criteria, the user can relax the constraints on the goal. Suppose that operations 4 and 5 are unavailable, operation 6 which is similar with excess (ExcessSim) to the request, may be the second possibility. It provides a subscription in addition to the weather report. The user may not be interested by this result if he is looking for a free service and if the subscription is a paying service. In another cases, he might be interested in additional outputs such as a list of weather reports for nearby cities, for example suppose now that the user is always searching for a weather report, but he can only provide a zip code.

Table 1. Six operations labeled with their input and output parameters sets.

	Input Parameters		Output Parameters
1	I1={ZIP}	1	O1={CITY-NAME}
2	I2 ={ZIP, GEOGRAPHICALREGION}	2	O2 ={CITY-NAME}
		3	O3={CITY-NAME, LONGITUDE, LATITUDE}
3	I3={ZIP}		
4	I4={ZIP}	4	O4={WEATHERREPORT}
5	I5 ={CITY-NAME}	5	O5={WEATHERREPORT}
6	I6 = {CITY-NAME}	6	O6 = {WEATHERREPORT, WEATHERREPORTSUBSCR}

When operation 4 is unavailable, then no operation can be found using FullSim, PartialSim or ExcessSim similarities. In this case, operation 5 can satisfy the need. It has a relational similarity (RelationSim) with the request because its outputs are identical to the goal, but inputs have nothing in common. This operation cannot be used alone, but it can lead to the goal if it is composed with other operations. In this case, operation 1 can first be invoked and its output parameter, a city name, is used to invoke operation 5. It is important to highlight that the proposed similarity functions have been designed to be complementary. FullSim function is the best solution. Then, PartialSim, ExcessSim and RelationalSim functions can give satisfaction to specific situations that are directly related to the context, as we have seen in the example above.

3. Structure of the Similarity Networks

In this section, we present the Web services benchmark used in our experiment. Four similarity networks corresponding to the four similarity functions are built from these data. Then, we provide a global view of the networks and we make a comparison between the similarity networks components and the notion of domain used in Web service classification. Finally, concentrating on the components, we take a local point of view by studying and comparing the structure of the components from the different networks.

3.1. Data

The similarity networks are extracted from SAWSDL-TC [11]. This SAWSDL test collection comes from SemWebCentral, an open source development Web site for the semantic Web. SAWSDL-TC is a service retrieval collection to support the evaluation of the performance of SAWSDL semantic Web service matchmaking algorithms. Although it has not been designed to test Web services substitution models, it best suits our requirements. It is partially composed of real-world Web services that are semantically described. The sets of Web services with similar functionalities are large enough to form reasonable communities. It contains 894 single operation descriptions and 654 are classified into 7 domains. Among them, economy, education and travel, contain more than 80% of the descriptions. Communication, food, medical and weapon contain the remaining 20% and their content is relatively uniform, economy, education, travel and communication are respectively organized into 10, 5, 6 and 2 sub-domains.

3.2. Global Structure

Whatever the similarity function used, the networks exhibit the same structure. A set of small components stand along with isolated nodes. Table 2 presents the number of components and proportion of isolated nodes of the networks. Isolated nodes are quite numerous in all the networks. According to these results, we can distinguish two types of networks. The first one includes the FullSim, PartialSim and ExcessSim networks while RelationSim is on the second group. Indeed, in the former the networks exhibit similar basic properties. PartialSim presents the lowest proportion of isolated nodes followed by ExcessSim then Fullsim. This behavior is in accordance with the restrictions imposed by the similarity definitions. In other words, there are more Web services that share common output and common inputs than Web services with exactly the same outputs. The differences observed between PartialSim and ExcessSim is probably due to a tougher constraint on the inputs in the later. Similarly, the number of components is quite comparable. Compared to the networks in the first group, RelationSim is quite different. It has at least two times less isolated nodes and the number of components is two times higher. This result suggests that there are a lot of operations that can be used in a substitution process through a composition. It implies to provide other operations to make the connection between the inputs of the desired operation and the inputs of the one extracted from the RelationSim network.

Table. 2. Basic Properties of the Similarity Networks

	FullSim	PartialSim
% isolated nodes	75%	57%
Nb of components	42	59

	ExcessSim	RelationSim
% isolated nodes	62%	31%
Nb of components	66	121

Note that the distribution of the operations does not reflect the organization of the collection into domains. This structure rather reflects the decomposition of the collection into a reasonable number of sets of similar operations. This is an interesting property. This observation reveals that the notion of domain is therefore not relevant for substitution. Note that if networks had been composed only of isolated nodes or if we had observed the presence of a giant component, those situations will have led to an inefficient distribution of the operations.

3.3. Local Structure

In order to have a more detailed idea on the influence of the different similarity functions on the networks topology, we investigate and compare the structure of the components. Results show that we can distinguish two types of networks according to the local structure as shown in Figure. 2a and 2b.

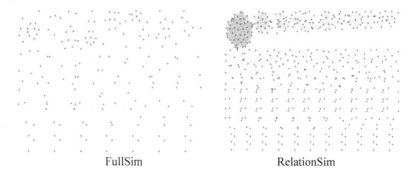

FullSim   RelationSim

Figure 2a. FullSim and RelationSim similarity networks where isolated nodes have been discarded.

In FullSim and RelationSim networks, components are organized into cliques, as shown in Figure. 2a. they are dominated by stars in PartialSim and ExcessSim networks, as we can see in Figure. 2b. The four networks are presented without their set of isolated nodes.

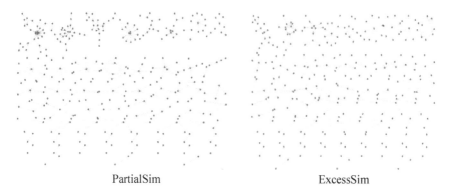

PartialSim   ExcessSim

Figure 2b. PartialSim and ExcessSim similarity networks where isolated nodes have been discarded

3.3.1. Clique as Basic Pattern

The clique basic pattern in the FullSim and RelationSim networks give rise to different situations. To illustrate this feature, we present three components of the FullSim network. The first one is shown on Figure. 3. It contains the get_BOOK and getEBook operations which form a 4-clique. They all produce a single parameter, Book, and they share at least one input parameter. The getEbook operations signatures are identical while getBook and getEbook have one common input parameter (Title). This component includes operations that are all similar according to the FullSim definition. They are all substitutable. If one wants to choose one of them for substitution, they can be distinguishable by their QoS features.

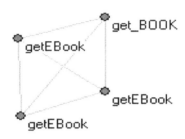

	getEBook	getBOOK
Input parameters	Title, User	Title
Output parameters	Book	Book

Figure 3. 4-clique FullSim network component and its operations' signature.

The second component on Figure. 4 contains six operations named get_LENDING. They are organized as follow: two 3-cliques and one 2-clique. The six operations have a single and same output parameter (Lending). On the right side of the figure, the links between the six operations are labeled by the concept of the input parameters shared by two adjacent operations. Unlike in the previous case, operations in this component are not all similar according to the Fullsim definition. Only operations that are within a clique follow this definition. This component includes three sets of similar operations which are organized into cliques. Two operations that are not in the same clique are similar according to the RelationSim definition. They have common outputs but their inputs do not overlap. Hence, when searching for substitutable operations in a FullSim component, all the cliques must be considered independently.

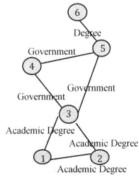

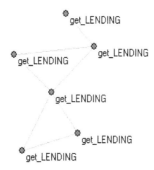

Figure 4: component of the FullSim network with 3 cliques (on the right side, the links' labels are the common inputs of two adjacent operations).

The third component shown in Figure. 5 contains thirteen operations named get_PRICE. They are organized in five cliques (one 6-clique, one 4-clique, one 3-clique, two 2-cliques). Sets of operations provide prices with overlapping inputs in each set.

Figure 5. FullSim network component with 5 cliques (1 6-clique, 1 4-clique, 1 3-clique and 2 2-cliques).

In the FullSim network, two components aggregate get_PRICE operations. Some get_PRICE operations also appear among the isolated nodes. get_PRICE operations are numerous in the collection. They belong to the economy domain where Web services are divided into different sub-categories (book, food, car, electronic device). The distribution of the operations among components seems to reflect these categories.

Distribution of similar operations within components allows classifying them according to their functionality. A component is a set of operations that have identical outputs. Operations with at least one common input are grouped within cliques in this component. A component is not a monolithic block of similar operations. It can be decomposed into a set of communities characterized by a clique. The clique pattern in the components allows a finer characterization of the notion of community of operations. Note that in the RelationSim network, the clique organization is more pronounced than in the FullSim network and some big components form a complete graph.

3.3.2. Star as Basic Pattern

The structure of the components in PartialSim and ExcessSim networks clearly differs from the previous ones. Whereas FullSim and RelationSim components are clique-like, PartialSim and ExcessSim components are rather organized as stars. We consider the PartialSim network in order to illustrate the most typical situations observed in these cases. Figure 6 shows a star component of the PartialSim network. The get_FILM central operation produces less output parameters compared to the peripheral operations. It produces only the parameter Film while the five others produce additional ones. It also has common input parameters with the peripheral operations. In this case, these six operations share a unique parameter (Title). The peripheral operations have a unique and same potential substitute. This substitute, which is pointed by the others, can replace them being aware that it provides less output that may be desired

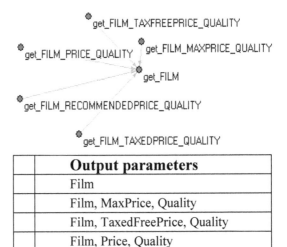

	Output parameters
	Film
	Film, MaxPrice, Quality
	Film, TaxedFreePrice, Quality
	Film, Price, Quality
	Film, Recommended Price, Quality
	Film, Taxed Price, Quality

Figure 6. Six -nodes star-like component of the PartialSim network and the output parameters of its operations.

Figure. 7 shows a component with 15 nodes made up with nested stars. Four operations may be replaced by others: get_DESTINATION_HOTEL, get_ACTIVITY_HOTEL, and two get_SPORTS_HOTEL operations. Unlike in the previous example, this component contains several substitutes. Some may replace only one operation; the get_HOTEL at the left end side is only a substitute for get_ACTIVITY_HOTEL. Others may replace several operations; all the get_HOTEL operations of the right end side can be substitutes for get_DESTINATION_HOTEL and the two get_SPORTS_HOTEL operations. Similarly than for the clique pattern encountered previously, the concept of similarity can be refined within a component. It occurs when the component does not simply contain a simple basic pattern, but a more complex structure built from this pattern.

In the example of Figure. 7, all the operations belong to the same classification domain. In this case, this is the travel domain. This is not always the case. They may also belong to different domains. The component made up with get_FUNDING operations on Figure. 8 illustrate this case. In this 24 nodes component, operations in columns labeled 'a' and 'b' come from the weapon domain. Those in the column labeled "*d*" are from the education domain.

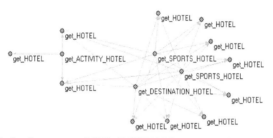

Figure 7. 15-Nodes Component Of The PARTIALSIM Network With Nested Stars.

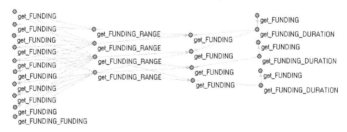

Figure 8 24 Nodes Component of the PARTIALSIM Network. All operations do not belong to the same domain.

Finally, those in the column labeled 'c' are from the education domain and they have a common input parameter with two of the get_FUNDING_RANGE operations and with one of the get_FUNDING_DURATION operations. Hence, within a same component, subsets can be based on different domains. In other words, the concept of similarity can be refined within the component. However, the criterion on which domains are made can be different. This will lead to different classifications of Web services. Indeed, the weapon domain and the education-governmentdegree_scholarship_service subdomain of education domain, from which the operations contained in this component come, may be grouped in a single domain. Both relate to government organizations funding, and this is what brings them together in the same component.

Let's now compare the PartialSim and ExcessSim networks throughout the examples of Figure. 5 and Figure. 7. When observing the same components in the ExcessSim network, they differ in two points. The links are oppositely oriented and some of them disappear if one operation has more input parameters than the one to which it is compared.

4. Conclusion

In this work, we have proposed a model to represent the functional similarity between Web services. The model is a network based approach in which similarity relationships between Web services operations functionalities are computed on their input and output parameters sets. We defined a set of four functions that represent different degrees of similarity between operations.

To evaluate this model, we have extracted four similarity networks from SAWSDL-TC1. Each network is based on one of the four similarity function. We analyzed and compared the structure of the networks. This comparative study shows that the networks share the same global structure. They are characterized by a large number of isolated nodes. It evolves from 30% to 75% depending on the more or less restrictive definition of similarity function. The remaining nodes are organized into a number of small components of similar operations. From the components analysis, we identified two classes of networks. The first class encompasses the FullSim and RelationSim networks in which the organizational basic pattern is the clique. In the second class, PartialSim and ExcessSim networks are organized around a star pattern.

In clique structured networks, a component is a clique or a set of cliques. In a FullSim component, all the operations of a clique have identical output parameters and their input parameters overlap. Two operations that do not belong to the same clique have disjoint input parameters. In some cases, the way operations are distributed among components seems to reflect the categories of the collection. We observed that in the RelationSim network, components are strongly connected and can be complete graphs.

In the star structured networks, a component is a star or a set of stars. In a PartialSim component, operations that are pointed by a link have less output parameters than the operations pointing toward them. Two linked operations have overlapping input parameters. Two operations that do not belong to the same star have disjoint input parameters. In an ExcessSim component, links are oppositely directed compared to the same component in the PartialSim network. Additionally, some links disappear because of the restriction on the input parameters sets. Components made of sets of stars reveal the presence of operations originating from different domains.

This proposed classification reveals two levels of similarity. The first one is the component and the second one is the component basic pattern (clique or star). A basic pattern within a component is a community that groups a set of similar and substitutable operations. This representation allows better understanding the functional similarity relationships that occur between Web services' operations. We plan to conduct thorough experiments to study the effectiveness of the proposed similarity networks to discover and substitute Web services during the composition process.

Summary

The diversity of users' needs and the ever growing number of Web services makes the discovering of the appropriate ones a challenging issue. In order to enhance the composition life cycle, an efficient organization of the Web services landscape must be integrated within discovery and substitution mechanisms. Classically, Web services are organized into non-overlapping categories based on a similarity metric. The main drawback of this approach is that it lacks the precise information that is needed toward Web service selection within a category. In this paper, we propose a finer organization based on networks. The nodes of the networks are the operations of the Web services while the links join similar operations. Four similarity measures based on the comparison of input and output parameters values of Web services operations are presented. A comparative evaluation of the topological structure of the corresponding networks is performed on a benchmark of semantically annotated Web services. Results show that, with this approach, we get a deeper and more subtle vision of the functional similarities between Web services.

References

1. B. Medjahed and A. Bouguettaya: A Dynamic Foundational Architecture for Semantic Web Services, Distributed and Parallel Databases, Vol. 17, no. 2, pp. 179–206 (2005).
2. I. Arpinar, B. Aleman-Meza, and R. Zhang: Ontology-driven web services composition platform, Inf. Syst. E-Business Management, Vol. 3 (2005).
3. B. Benatallah, M. Dumas, and Q. Z. Sheng: Facilitating the Rapid Development and Scalable Orchestration of Composite Web Services, Distributed and Parallel Databases, Vol. 17, no. 1, pp. 5–37 (2005).
4. Y. Taher, D. Benslimane, M.-C. Fauvet, and Z. Maamar: Towards an Approach for Web Services Substitution, in 10th International Database Engineering and Applications Symposium, pp. 166–173 (2006).
5. A. Konduri and C. Chan: Clustering of Web Services Based on WordNet Semantic Similarity, University of Akron, USA, Akron (2008).
6. R. Nayak and B. Lee: Web Service Discovery with additional Semantics and Clustering, in IEEE/WIC/ACM International Conference on Web Intelligence, pp. 555–558 (2007).
7. Z. Azmeh, M. Huchard, C. Tibermacine, C. Urtado, and S. Vauttier: WSPAB: A Tool for Automatic Classification & Selection of Web Services Using Formal Concept Analysis, in Sixth European Conference on Web Services, pp. 31–40 (2008).

8. U. Keller, R. Lara, H. Lausen, A. Polleres, and D. Fensel: Automatic Location of Web Services, ESWC. Heraklion, Crete, Greece (2005).
9. U. Küster and B. König-Ries: Evaluating semantic web service matchmaking effec tiveness based on graded relevance, in Proc. of the 2nd International Workshop SMR2 on Service Matchmaking and Resource Retrieval in the Semantic Web at ISWC (2008).
10. M. Paolucci, T. Kawamura, T. R. Payne, and K. Sycara: Semantic Matching of Web Services Capabilities, in The Semantic Web - ISWC2002 - LNCS, Vol. 2342, pp. 333–347 (2002).
11. SemWebCentral.org, 2008. [Online]. Available: http://projects.semwebcentral.org/projects/sawsdl-tc/.

Chapter 3

Measuring Cognitive Load for Visualizations in Learning Computer Programming Physiological Measures

1. Introduction

The first section discusses the experimental set up used to monitor the cognitive load and the second section discusses on the experimental design for the experiments. The third section of the paper discusses briefly on the signal interpretation of the EEG. The fourth section of the paper analyses the results of the experiment using EEG and final part summarizes to end with the overall discussion on the experiments. The main contribution from the paper will be to report on the suitability of the EEG measure for measuring cognitive load and also to determine whether the visualization tool really helps in reducing the cognitive load.

2. Experimental Setup

We already mentioned to use EEG as indicator of cognitive load. The device for the purpose of measuring cognitive load was identified. The device that was used in our study is Procomp Infiniti biofeedback device [5]. A brief idea on the device is given below. The hardware component includes

- One encoder unit (ProComp Infiniti)
- One TT-USB interface unit
- A supply of fiber optic cable
- Four alkaline AA Batteries.

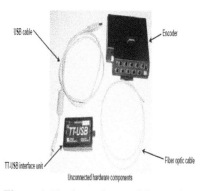

Figure 1. Hardware Setup of the Device

2.1. Sensors

The experimental setup consists of sensors which is useful to measure the feedback.

Feedback is measured using any one of the following sensors

- EEG Z Sensor or EEG Flex or Pro sensor
- GSR Sensor

2.2. EEG-Z Sensor

The EEG-Z is a pre-amplified electroencephalograph sensor with built in impedance sensing capabilities. This sensor can be toggled to record regular EEG or monitor skin impedance (both the reactive and resistive elements) to help optimize electrode hook-up. It can be used for assessment and EEG biofeedback. Each EEG-Z sensor comes with a monopolar/bipolar electrode kit shown in the figure below(Infiniti 2009)

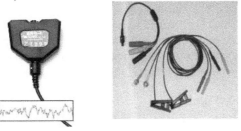

Figure 2. EEG Sensor of the Device

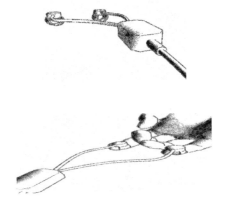

Figure 3. Skin Conductance Sensor

2.3. Software for EEG (Electrooculography)

The software used in recording the feedback.
- Biography infiniti software
- EEG Suite

The following figure 3 [15] shows the introductory screen of the biograph infiniti software.

Figure 4. Screenshot of the Biograph Infiniti

The load is monitored by using the Bio Feedback device Procomp Infiniti by observing the EEG signals.

3. Experimental Design

The aim of the experiment is to measure the cognitive load by using various visualization techniques. It is widely believed that the visualization is expected to reduce the load experienced due to the fact that using visualization expands working memory and thereby reducing the cognitive load during the learning process. In this experiment the students are exposed to different visualizations by using different visualization tools namely Jeliot [7], Ville [9] and Teaching Machine.

The experiment was conducted at University of Malaya, Kuala Lumpur with a group of students doing the introductory programming course. All the students were expected to be having the same level of knowledge in terms of programming and most of them are novice programmers. The number of students who took part in the experiment was eleven. Each of these students was made to learn different concepts of programming using different visualization tools. When the learning takes place EEG recordings will be carried out using the Procomp Infiniti device and Biograph infiniti software. In addition to using the visualization systems some experiments were conducted by handing over the programs in a piece of paper manually and try to understand the code and during that process also the EEG readings will be recorded. This is done to analyze the difference between the use of visualization and normal mode of learning programming.

Table 1 explains the test bed of experiments used. The sampling is done in such a way every student is exposed to different visualization tool and at the same time taking into consideration that the learners come across different concepts.

Table 4 Test Experiment Parameters

Concept of Programming	Position	Visualization Tools		
		ViLLE	**Jeliot**	**Teaching Machine**
Variable declaration	C	1,4,7,10	2,5,8,11	3,6,9
Conditional statements	F	1,4,7,10	2,5,8,11	3,6,9
Looping statements	P	1,4,7,10	2,5,8,11	3,6,9
Functions	C	2,5,8,11	3,6,9	1,4,7,10
Functions call by values	F	2,5,8,11	3,6,9	1,4,7,10
Simple Array program	P	2,5,8,11	3,6,9	1,4,7,10
Difficult Array program	C	3,6,9	1,4,7,10	2,5,8,11
Factorial program using recursion	F	3,6,9	1,4,7,10	2,5,8,11
Difficult program of recursion using Towers of Hanoi	P	3,6,9	1,4,7,10	2,5,8,11
Sorting program	C	1,4,7,10	2,5,8	3,6,9

In the above table, the number in each visualization column indicates the subjects and position indicates the placement of the EEG-Z sensor in different parts of the cerebral hemisphere. The following Figure 4 gives an overview of the placement of the sensors during the process of the experiment.

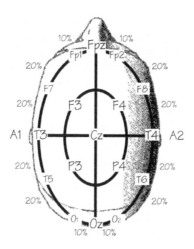

Figure 5a. Placement of Electrodes for EEG measurement

In our experiments the sensors were placed in the points C4, F4 and P4.The points were/ taken as standard to ensure the consistency of the results.

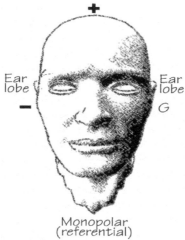

Figure 5b. Placement of Electrodes for EEG measurement

4. Interpretation of the EEG Signals

EEG waves are very of different types. They are differentiated based on their frequency. Each wave reflects various states of the human brain. So in this study it becomes vital to interpret the EEG signals. Table 2 explains about the various types of EEG waves and their interpretation [4]. In our experiment the results are interpreted using the pattern of alpha, beta, gamma waves. More intellectual or problem solving activity will suppress the emergence of alpha wave and emergence of beta and gamma waves. So we assume that the increase of alpha means results in cognitive load as the mind goes to idling state. On the contrary the increase of beta and gamma mean that the student is focused and involved in mental activity [16]. A total of 121 experiments were conducted. Each experiment was given to different subjects using different visualizations and with a fixed time quantum of 15 minutes. The next section, we analyze the results using the two different approaches namely

- Concept wise analysis.
- Student wise analysis.

5. Results –Concept Wise

The following graphs illustrate the alpha, beta and gamma frequency for different concepts using different visualization tools. The first concept of variable declaration which was considered by many students as the easy concept based on the survey done. The results are indicated in chart 1. All the students were given paper and try to understand the program. But it is found irrespective of the same system difference alpha, beta and gamma values are recorded for various students. The highest value for gamma and beta was recorded for the subject 8 .The alpha value was lowest for the first subject. This shows that the uniformity does not exist

Table 2. Interpretation of EEG Signals

Types of Waves	Frequency	State of Mind – Inference
Alpha	8-12 Hz	• State of Relaxation and represent brain shifting into a idling gear • Shows a state of bit relaxed and disengaged. • Closing eyes for half a minute can cause more generation of alpha waves.
Beta	Above 13 Hz	• State of Intellectual activity and outwardly focused concentration. • It shows state of alertness – Bright eyed and bushy tailed
Theta	4-8 Hz	• State of day dream like • Associated with mental in efficiency
Delta	0.5 to 3.5 Hz	• Slowest and highest amplitude wave – representing a sleep like scenario • When brain goes offline • Drowsy and having learning disabilities • When excessive waves are present it becomes difficult to control attention, behavior of humans.
Gamma		• Gamma waves is associated with problem solving, higher mental activity. It is indicative of attentiveness of sensory stimulation

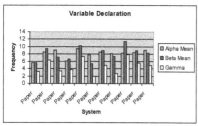

Chart 1: Results for the concept variable declaration

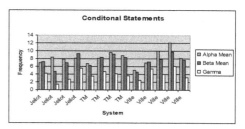

Chart 2: Results for the concept conditional statement

in the level of difficulty irrespective of the same system and same concept been attempted. Chart 2 indicates the alpha, beta and gamma for the concept of looping. The first four subjects used Jeliot, followed by four subjects using TM and five other subjects used Ville. The consistency was not observed in the patterns of the means of the alpha, beta and gamma even while using the same system .The chart 3 indicates the alpha, beta, gamma means for the concept of the conditional statements. A strong co relation exists between beta and gamma waves. Beta and gamma waves tend to increase or decrease proportionally in most cases.

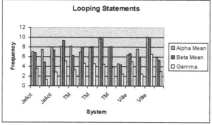

Chart 3. Results for the concept looping statements

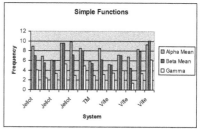

Chart 4. Results for the concept simple functions

Chart 5. Results for the concept function-call by values

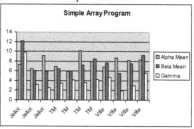

Chart 6. Results for the concept simple array program

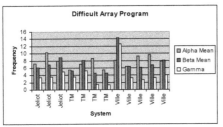

Chart 7. Results for the concept difficult array program

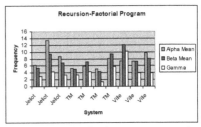

Chart 8. Results for the concept recursion

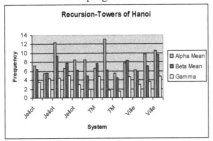

Chart 9. Results for the concept recursion-Towers of Hanoi

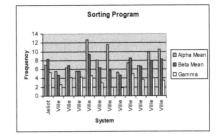

Chart 10. Results for the concept sorting program

Chart 4 indicates the EEG recording for the concept of simple functions and Chart 5 indicates the alpha, beta and gamma means for the concept of function-call by value. Even though the concept is similar to one another, there is a variation in the mean of alpha, beta and gamma while using across different systems. Even when using the same system we observe variations between each learner. The chart 6 and 7 indicates the values of alpha, beta, gamma for the concept of arrays. One program was simple and the other was little tedious form of using the array. In the case of simple array program highest beta and gamma mean was recorded when using the Jeliot system while Ville system recorded the highest beta and gamma means in the case of difficult array program. Chart 8 and 9 indicate the results of learning the concept of recursion. It was observed that the Ville showed higher beta and gamma values showing problem solving activity. Highest alpha value was recorded in Jeliot for recursion (factorial) program and in the case of recursion concept for towers of Hanoi program TM had the highest alpha value. Chart 10 indicates the results of the concept of sorting. In this concept most of the subjects experienced using the Ville system. It was found that the some subjects recorded the highest value for alpha while using Ville and highest beta value is recorded while using Ville and peak gamma was seen when using Eliot system. The results of the experiment is summarized as table as shown in Table 3.

6. Analysis of the Results –Concept Wise

We analyzed to see whether any pattern emerges from the results. This emergence of the pattern based on the results can help to understand the results properly. The alpha, beta and gamma wave means recorded during the experiment were considered for the possible patterns. The pattern is arrived by assigning the highest value mean as 1, the middle value mean as 2 and the least value mean as 3 for the three signals namely alpha, beta and gamma. The possible patterns are that alpha mean is the highest, followed by the beta mean and lastly the gamma mean. These are indicated by 1, 2, and 3.The other possible patterns are 2, 1, 3 with beta mean in the highest, alpha mean in the second lowest and the gamma mean in the lowest. The last possible pattern is 3, 1, 2 where the gamma mean is the highest, followed by the alpha mean and lastly by beta mean. The following table 4 shows the available patterns and the indications of the cognitive load.

After analyzing the results we have summarized the results for various concepts on the basis of the patterns of Alpha, Beta and Gamma mean as discussed in table 5.4. The following table 5.5 indicates the number of occurrences of the patterns for each concept. We can infer from the above table 5.5 that for many concepts, the learners experienced high cognitive load during the process of learning. There are cases where the student actually experienced low cognitive load, resulting in learning only in the case of the two concepts namely difficult array and factorial program. In most of the other cases, the cognitive load has always remained high either with students seemed to be in relaxed mind without any focus and effort or the students having tried to focus on the learning. The learning did not take place in both the cases due to the high cognitive load. The concept function is difficult among all the concepts as there are around twelve students with the pattern 1, 2, 3.The negligible presence of the pattern 3, 1, 2 for high value means of Alpha, Beta and Gamma waves stands testimony for this argument

Table 3. Results of EEG experiment concept wise

Concept of Programming	Alpha Mean		Beta Mean		Gamma Mean	
	High	Low	High	Low	High	Low
Variable declaration	9.748	5.621	11.44	5.375	7.868	1.976
	Paper	Paper	Paper	Paper	Paper	Paper
Conditional statements	12.14	5.025	9.815	4.582	6.098	1.354
	Ville	Ville	Ville	Ville	Ville	Jeliot
Looping statements	10.092	4.579	9.978	4.354	6.553	1.356
	Ville	Ville	Ville	Ville	Ville	Jeliot
Functions	9.878	5.272	10.053	4.464	6.239	1.472
	Jeliot	Ville	Ville	Ville	Ville	Ville
Functions call by values	10.298	5.695	11.321	5.201	7.071	1.885
	Ville	Ville	Ville	Ville	Ville	Ville

Simple Array program	10.206	5.843	12.149	5.476	9.865	1.924
	TM	TM	Ville	Jeliot	Jeliot	Ville
Difficult Array program	10.337	5.407	14.318	4.548	12.592	1.303
	Jeliot	TM	Ville	TM	Ville	TM
Factorial program using recursion	13.457	5.093	12.095	4.333	10.241	1.394
	Jeliot	TM	Ville	TM	Ville	TM
Difficult program of recursion using Towers of Hanoi	13.103	5.468	9.623	4.438	5.026	1.476
	TM	TM	Ville	TM	Jeliot	TM
Sorting program	12.674	5.386	9.458	4.739	5.345	1.867
	Ville	Ville	Ville	Ville	Jeliot	Ville

Table 4. Patterns Based on the Results of EEG experiment

Alpha Mean	Beta Mean	Gamma Mean	Interpretation	State of Cognitive Load
1	2	3	Alpha is high. Beta is in middle Gamma is in least	Cognitive Load is high and thereby no learning takes place
2	1	3	Alpha is middle. Beta is high Gamma is in least	Cognitive Load is still high and there is an effort from the learner to focus on learning.
3	1	2	Alpha is low. Beta is high. Gamma is in middle	Cognitive load is less and actual learning takes place

7. Experiment Results-Student Wise

The following table 6 tabulates the experiment results on the basis of the students. When we analyze the results from the table above we can infer that the same student experience different measure of alpha, beta, and gamma means even in

Table 5. Results of EEG Experiment Concept Wise

Concept of Programming	Pattern of Alpha,Beta,Gamma Mean		
	1 2 3	2 1 3	3 1 2
Variable declaration	6	5	0
Conditional statements	8	4	0
Looping statements	8	5	0
Functions	12	1	0
Functions call by values	7	4	0
Simple Array program	6	5	0
Difficult Array program	6	4	1
Factorial program using recursion	6	3	1

Difficult program of recursion using Towers of Hanoi	9	4	0
Sorting program	9	3	0

Table 6. Experiment Results-Student Wise

	Alpha Mean		Beta Mean		Gamma Mean	
	High	Low	High	Low	High	Low
Student 1	8.911	4.579	7.707	4.354	4.827	2.448
Student 2	8.617	5.199	9.479	4.928	6.33	3.414
Student 3	7.466	5.932	9.084	6.674	5.345	3.622
Student 4	12.141	5.851	10.275	5.369	7.409	2.94
Student 5	13.103	6.728	6.213	4.464	2.007	1.354
Student 6	8.517	5.695	14.318	5.201	12.592	3.057
Student 7	9.851	7.468	11.44	8.388	7.868	4.27
Student 8	9.592	6.235	9.558	5.978	5.568	2.956
Student 9	9.878	9.188	9.702	5.924	4.522	2.466
Student 10	10.561	7.771	9.623	7.536	5.616	3.457
Student 11	13.457	6.844	9.476	5.537	4.556	2.414

case the same visualization is used. This makes us to conclude that the same visualization does not reduce the cognitive load in a similar way for all the concepts. Some visualization helps in reducing the load in some concepts while it does not in other concepts. These variations in the patterns are due the levels of the concepts according to the difficulty level. Bloom's taxonomy refers to the levels of concepts according to the levels of difficulty. From table 6 above, we can infer that the same student experiences different measure of alpha, beta, and gamma means even in case the same visualization is used. We conclude that the same type of visualization does not reduce the cognitive load in a similar way for all the concepts. Some visualization helps in reducing the load in some cases while it does not help in other cases. Other factors such the level of the concept which is learnt, may also have an impact on the cognitive load which is similar to the classification of the concepts based on the difficulty level as stated in Bloom's taxonomy. This means that certain visualization will help only for certain concepts

Table 7. Patterns of EEG experiment - Student wise

Student	EEG Pattern		
	1 2 3	2 1 3	3 2 1
Student 1	12	1	0
Student 2	3	7	0
Student 3	10	0	0
Student 4	2	8	0
Student 5	9	1	0
Student 6	10	0	0
Student 7	3	3	2
Student 8	10	0	0

Student 9	0	10	0
Student 10	5	5	0
Student 11	10	0	0

The results of the experiments are summarized on the pattern of the means of alpha, beta, gamma waves recorded during the experiments. We adopted the same method of arriving at patterns as we did before. The table 4 can be referred for the interpretation of the pattern. The following table 7 indicates the patterns based on alpha, beta and gamma waves for each student who took part in the experiments. From table 7, we can infer that out of the eleven students who took part in the experiments, most of the students have experienced higher cognitive load. Some of the students experienced higher cognitive load and their mind became relaxed due to higher cognitive load and there was no focus in learning. This was the case with the six out of the eleven students .The students 1, 3, 5, 6, 8 and 11 fell under this category. There were other students who also experienced higher cognitive load but still tried to focus on learning. Also there were three students namely 2, 4, 9 in this category and only student namely 7 who had experienced lesser cognitive load and involved in problem solving and understanding the concept.

8. Galvanic Skin Response Experiment

Another experiment was conducted by using Skin Conductance as an index of cognitive load. The main objective of this experiment is to find the feasibility of using another physiological measure of cognitive load which is Skin Conductance (SC) which is also called as Galvanic Skin Response (GSR).The experimental setup is same as before in experiment 1. The only change in setup is that we connected the Skin Conductance (SC) sensor to monitor the skin conductance mean for every experiment. In this experiment seven subjects took part. Each of these subjects were given three programs namely Function call by value, Difficult Array program and Recursion and they experienced learning using the ViLLE Visualization system.The results of the experiment are discussed in the following section.

8.1. Experiment Results

The results of the three experiments are shown in the following graphs .The graphs shows the skin conductance mean for the three different concepts namely function program-call by values, difficult array program and recursion. Table 8 summarizes the experiment results.

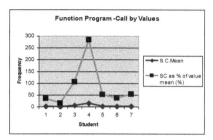

8(a)

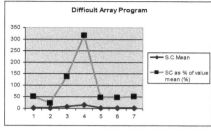

8(b)

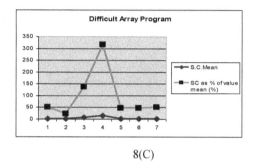

8(C)

Table 8. GSR Experiment results

Concept of Programming	S.C.Mean		S.C. as % of value mean %	
	High	**Low**	**High**	**Low**
Function call by values	14.148	0.691	282.955	13.82
Difficult Array Program	15.785	1.119	315.695	22.387
Recursion	14.748	2.017	294.961	40.348

In the above experiment, the same type of visualization was used for all the subjects. It is found that irrespective of using the same type of visualization and the same programming concept, the cognitive load experienced is different. For example in the case of the functional call by values program had the highest S.C Mean as 14.148 and the lowest as 0.691.It marks an enormous variation among the subjects who took part in the same conditions of experiment with the same visualization tool and the same programming concept. This variation could be due to the background knowledge of the students and the individual learning style. The same applies to all other concepts. So we conclude that the GSR is not reliable in normal class room settings, as GSR levels experienced vary for all the subjects. This variation is caused by many external factors. Although some prior researches have used measures like GSR as an index of cognitive load, it cannot be used in a normal class room setting. This variation of the GSR may be attributed to the different levels of knowledge possessed by the students and the background about the knowledge and skill related to programming for various students. It is the assumption that all the students are of same level and they are novice whereas in reality, the students' level of knowledge and skills varies as mentioned before.

9. Conclusion

As mentioned earlier, most of the visualization system are monotonous and does not provide room for user interaction at time when the learners faces difficulty. The choice of the visualization tool to the learning is done randomly. Cognitive Load Theory (CLT) also considers the long term memory schema of the learners. The Long Term Memory (LTM) may be different for each learners as they have different levels of expertise in domains related to programming such as mathematics, analogy etc. In our experiment we also employed the rating scale of 10 to rate the difficulty of learning by the learners. It is found that there is no proportionality between the rating difficulties expressed by non-physiological measures to that of the physiological measures. This lack of co relation might be due to the frustration experienced by the subjects due to the fixing of electrodes. It is also observed that the students tend to increase their alpha mean when the same system is given consequently. This is due to the reason that they become more relaxed as they are getting familiar with the same system and also they get bored due to the same type of visualizations. It is also our conclusion that visualizations do help in reducing the difficulty of learning .But what we see from the results is that all visualizations are not equally effective in reducing the load. Some visualization is not clearly understood by the novices and it increases the load.

Physiological measures are expected to be better indicator of cognitive load since the measures are monitored without the knowledge of the learner. This is quite contrary to the non-physiological measures that are used traditionally to monitor cognitive load. In non-physiological measures the cognitive load is measured based on the user's feedback. It is found that not all visualizations are not equally helpful in helping to reduce cognitive. Some students found the reduction of load using certain visualizations for certain concepts. Some visualization did not help in reducing the load for some concepts. A mechanism to monitor the load and customize the instruction by using different visualizations could help further in reducing the cognitive load. This optimization could be implemented using techniques like Artificial Neural Network. This optimization becomes necessary as the cognitive load reduction is not uniform for all students and same concepts. On the other hand when the results are analyzed on the basis of the concepts using the different visualization tools we also infer that it is difficult to conclude that a certain visualization tool is effective in reducing the cognitive load. This is due to the reason the cognitive load could increase for certain students when they are newly introduced to visualization tools. It is also to be taken into consideration that all novices are not same as they have varied levels of background and associated skills of learning programming.

The results of the experiment also helped us to conclude that physiological measures like EEG could not be a good indicator for cognitive load in a normal class room setting. It may be suitable to use the physiological measures in a controlled experimental setting. The participants faced some difficulties to fix the wire and many learners were not happy that the experiment involves fixing of electrodes in their head. It was quite a difficult task to motivate the students in taking part in the experiments. This type of experimental setup for observing or analyzing the cognitive load created a stress and some learners experienced frustration. Another important factor that needs to be addressed in the effort of measuring cognitive load is the background of mathematical skills possessed by the learners. This is due to the fact that mathematics and computer programming have a strong correlation and the background of mathematical skills, analogy, problem solving and the ability to perform in mathematics should also be considered in order to find how effective the visualizations could reduce the cognitive load. The consideration of this factor can attribute to the Cognitive load theory which also considers the long term memory and that is attributed by the prior knowledge related to the learning and it is represented in the form of schemas. So the study has helped to report the suitability of using EEG for measuring cognitive load. The study also helped to find out how effective the visualization tool in reduces the cognitive load.

Summary

Computer programming is a complex skill to acquire for novice learners who are in their initial phase of learning programming. There are many factors that results in difficulties in learning programming. This paper addresses to resolve one core difficulty which is cognitive load [2] [3].Cognitive load theory [13] is a famous theory of learning. It states that the schema of the long term memory is not well built in the case of novices and also there is a limitation of working memory's capacity. This makes it hard for novices to understand the concepts and equip with the skills necessary to become programmers. Some efforts used to overcome the cognitive load are the visualization tools for learning programming [14] .There is no accountability on how effective these visualization systems helped in reducing the load. The mechanism to measure cognitive load is not used in the visualization systems. There are two methods of cognitive load measurement namely physiological and non-physiological measures. Physiological measures include EKG,GSR[12],EEG[11],Temperature[11] etc. and non-physiological measures includes rating scale[6] and some recent research studies have used EEG as an index for cognitive load measurement [7].We felt that using the physiological measures could be accurate as they are the reflections of the body impulses. There is no user's control over the measurement. We also decided to use EEG as the latest efforts of measuring the cognitive uses EEG. The study also employed one more physiological measure namely GSR. This paper addresses the cognitive load measurement while using visualization tools by the novice programmers using EEG and GSR as an index of cognitive load.

References

1. A.Badley, G. H. (2008). "Baddley's model of working memory." Retrieved July 2008, from http://en.wikipedia.org/wiki/Baddeley%27s_model_of_working_memory.
2. Garner, S. (2002). Reducing the Cognitive Load on Novice Programmers. ED-MEDIA World Conference on Educational Multimedia & Telecommunications, Denver, Coloroda, Association for the advancement of computing in Education.
3. Gomes, A. and A. J. Mendes (2007). Learning to program-difficulties and solutions. International conference on Engineering Education - ICEE 2007. Coimbra, Portugal.
4. Hammond, D. C. (2004). "A introduction to Neurofeedback." Journal of Neuro Therapy.
5. Infiniti, P. (2009). "Procomp Infiniti Hardware Manual." Retrieved July, 2008, from
   http://www.thoughttechnology.com/pdf/manuals/SA7510%20Rev%206.pdf
6. Paas, F., J. E.Tuovinen, et al. (2003). "Cognitive Load Measurement as a means to Advance Cognitive Load Theory." Educational Psyhchologist 38(1): 63-71.
7. Pavlo Antonenko et.al. (2010). Using Electroencephalography to Measure Cognitive Load.Educ Psychol Rev 22:425–438
8. R.Ben-Bassat Levy, M. B.-A., P.A.Uronen (2003). "The Jeliot 2000 program animation system." Education 40(1): 1-15.
9. Rajala, T., et.al, (2007). VILLE- MultiLanguage Tool for Teaching Novice Programming. TUCS Technical Report TUCS.
10. Rajala, T., Laakso, M-J., Kaila,E and Salakoski,T. (2008). "Effectiveness of Program Visualization: A Case Study with the ViLLE Tool." Journal of Information Technology Education: Innovations in Practice 7: 15-32.
11. S.Ikehara, C. and M. E.Crosby (2005). Assessing Cognitive Load with Physiological sensors. 38th Hawaii International Conference on System Sciences 2005, Hawaii, USA.
12. Shi, Y. (2007). Galvanic Skin Response (GSR) as an index of Cognitive Load. CHI 2007, San Jose, CA, USA.
13. Sweller, J. (1988). "Cognitive load during problem solving: Effects on learning." Cognitive Science 12: 257-285.
14. Sweller, J. (2008). "Visualisation and Instructional Design." Retrieved January, from http://www.cmu.edu/teaching/trynew/sweller-visualinstructionaldesign.pdf.
15. Technology, T. (2008). "Getting Started with Biograph Infiniti." Retrieved January, from
    http://www.thoughttechnology.com/pdf/manuals/SA7951%20ver%205.1%20E EG%20Suite.pdf.
16. Wikipedia. (2009). "Electroencelography." Retrieved August, 2009, from http://en.wikipedia.org/wiki/Electroencephalography.

Chapter 4

Meta-Models In Support Of Database Model Transformations[1]

1. Introduction

The emergence of large and complex software systems increases the interest in Model-Driven Software Engineering (MDSE), as a way to lower the cost of development and maintenance of software. Models allow us to hide irrelevant details, provide different model viewpoints, and isolate and modularize models of cross-cutting concerns of a system under study. Models, as first class entities [26], are used to specify, simulate, test, verify and generate code for the application to be built [8]. Many of these activities include the specification and execution of model-to-model (M2M) or model-to-text (M2T) transformations. During these transformations model elements are traced from a more abstract model to a more concrete model and vice versa, achieved through meta-modeling [1]. A meta-model defines the modeling language, i.e. the constructs that can be used to make a model and, consequently, defines a set of valid models [4]. In that way the execution of M2M transformations of a model conformant to a meta-model into another one conformant to a different meta-model is facilitated. The most mature formulation of MDSE paradigm currently is the OMG's Model-Driven Architecture (MDA) which refers to a high-level description of an application as a Platform Independent Model (PIM) and a more concrete implementation-oriented description as a Platform Specific Model (PSM) [22]. The OMG's Meta Object Facility (MOF) defines the metadata architecture that lies at the heart of MDA.

MOF standard [20] offers a generic framework that combines both syntax and semantics of models and model transformations. MOF meta-modeling architecture is defined in a way that meta-models and models based on it can be linked together using a simple language. MOF is used to define semantics and structure of generic meta-models or domain specific ones. It provides a four-level hierarchy, with levels M0–M3. The concept of a model is specialized depending on the level, in which a model is located. Therefore it is: a model at M1 level, a meta-model at M2 level and a meta-meta-model at M3 level.

In MDSE generally, as well as in MDA in particular, models are not just designer artifacts, but they are included in production process meaning that a code

---

[1] Research presented in this paper was supported by Ministry of Science and Technological Development of Republic of Serbia, Grant III-44010, Title: *Intelligent Systems for Software Product Development and Business Support based on Models.*

---

for target platform may be generated from such models. These models differ in how much platform specific information they contain. A platform should not be seen just as an execution infrastructure. Atkinson and Kuhne in [5] a platform view *"as any system capable of supporting the fulfillment of some goal with respect to a software application"*. They emphasize that platform independency is not a binary property, and therefore one can view several PSMs, with different degree of platform independency. Therefore, a designer starts with a high-level model, abstracting from all kinds of platform issues. Through the chain of M2M transformations, ending up with a M2T transformation, initial PIM iteratively transforms to a series of PSMs with less independency degree, introducing more and more platform specific extensions.

Meta-modeling is widely spread area of research. Since software development process produces several models, going from abstract to concrete, there is a broad space of problems involving the design, integration and maintenance of complex application artifacts, such as application programs, databases, web sites and user interfaces (UI). Engineers use tools to manipulate models of these artifacts, such as class diagrams, interface definitions, database schemas, web site layouts, XML schemas, and UI form specifications.

In the paper we focus on models relating to databases. For these models we use the generic name **database models**.

A database is a collection of related data stored on some storage medium controlled by the database management system (DBMS). The description of database that is specified during database design is called **database schema**. A **data model** provides the means to achieve data abstraction and to express database schema. According to Date and Darwen definition [12] revised by Eessaar [13]: *"A data model is an abstract, self-contained, implementation-independent definition of elements of a 4-tuple of sets (T, S, O, C) that together make up the abstract machine with which database users interact, where T is a set of data types; S is a set of data structure types; O is a set of data operation types; C is a set of integrity constraint types."* Numerous data models are proposed. Elmasri and Navathe classify data models according to the types of concepts they use to describe the database structure, as follows: i) high-level or **conceptual data models**; ii) representational, logical or **implementation data models**, and iii) low-level or **physical data models** [15].

Some of the well-known data models are: hierarchical, network, entity-relationship (ER), extended ER (EER), relational, object-oriented and object-relational (OR). Some of them are used mostly for the conceptual database schema design (like ER and EER data models), while the others are used predominantly for logical and implementation database design and database implementation (like relational and OR data model). A database schema has to conform to a data model. A database management system (DBMS) is based on a data model, too. Hence, there are relational DBMS (RDBMS) and OR DBMS, e.g. the plethora of models related to databases points out to the need and importance of M2M and M2T transformations between these database models. Thereby, the abstraction level of target model of a transformation may be the same, lower or higher comparing to the abstraction level of source model. An explicit representation of mappings specifies how two models are related to each other. Some mapping examples, according to Bernstein [7] are: i) mapping between an entity-relationship (ER) model and a SQL schema to navigate between a database schema conceptual design and its implementation; ii) mapping between class definitions and relational schemas to generate object wrappers; iii) mapping between data sources and a mediated schema to drive heterogeneous data integration; iv) mapping between a database schema and its next release to guide data migration or view evolution, etc. Additionally, the growth of eXtended Markup Language (XML) technologies has led to the need to have object-oriented (OO) wrappers for XML data and the translation from nested XML documents into flat relational databases and vice versa.

In a forward engineering process there is a chain of M2M model transformations, ending up with M2T transformation that transform a conceptual database schema, via an implementation database schema and a physical database schema, into an SQL script e.g., aimed at creating database under the vendor specific RDBMS. The abstraction level of models is decreasing throughout the chain of transformations.

In a reverse engineering process the abstraction level of models is increasing throughout the chain of transformations. Starting from a physical database schema, recorded into RDBMS data repository e.g., a logical database schema (based on the relational data model) or a conceptual database schema (ER or EER database schema) could be extracted. Both of them are at the higher abstraction level than the physical database schema.

To manage heterogeneous data, many applications need to translate data and their descriptions from one model (i.e. data model) to another. Even small variations of models are often enough to create difficulties. For example, Structured Query Language (SQL) is currently available in most commercial and open-source RDBMSs. It is also the focus of a continuous standardization process, resulting in SQL standards (the current revision is: SQL: 2011, ISO/IEC 9075:2011). However, issues of SQL code portability between major RDBMS products still exist due to a lack of full compliance with the standard and proprietary vendor extensions. Therefore, even the mapping between SQL database schemas extracted from RDBMS data repository of different vendors may be a serious problem.

Model transformations between database models we call **database model transformations**. These transformations are based on meta-models that are confirmed by the source and target database models of the transformations. These meta-models are said to be **in support of database model transformation**. Due to the diversity of database models it is important to classify meta-models of database models and to distribute them across the abstraction level stack. In the paper we propose a classification of database meta-models. We have designed a meta-model of relational database schema based on the theoretical foundations of relational data model. It is presented in the paper to illustrate abundance and diversity of relational data model constructs, alongside with semantics that may be expressed in logical relational database schema.

In the purpose of specifying and managing our meta-model we use the Eclipse Modeling Framework (EMF) [14], a current MOF-like modeling environment. The EMF meta-modeling language is based on the Ecore meta-meta-model which is closely aligned with the Essential MOF (EMOF) specification [20].

2. A Classification of Database Meta-Models

The work we describe in this paper unifies two main research areas: database design and implementation and meta-modeling in the context of MDSE. We identify different kinds of database meta-models (MMs) that are models of modeling languages used to express database models at certain abstraction level. Hereof, we distinguish:

- data model meta-models;
- generic database schema meta-models:
    - generic conceptual database schema meta-models
    - generic logical database schema meta-models;
- standard physical database schema meta-models; and
- Vendor-specific physical database schema meta-models.

In Table 1 we propose a classification and distribution of database meta-models and database models across the MOF level stack. System under study (SUS) is at the M0 level. An SUS is represented by a model at M1 level, which conforms to a meta-model at M2 level that is conformant with a meta-meta-model at M3 level. For example, in column (5) in Table 1, a database instance may be represented by an Oracle 10g database schema conformant with the Oracle 10g database schema meta-model conformant with EMOF.

Data model meta-models stand at the M2 level of MOF stack. For example, one may specify relational data model meta-model or ER data model meta-model, and they are containing constructs like data types, data structure types, constraint types, etc. They are specific for relational or ER data model, respectively. In a generic approach we can assume that besides well-known data models may emerge new data models and their meta-models may be included in this classification. Some of the generic database schema meta-models describe conceptual database schemas, like ER or EER database schema MM, while others describe logical database schemas, like relational or OR database schema MM. In both cases they are based on theoretical foundations of ER/EER, relational or data model, respectively.

Relational data model is the focus of continues standardization process, and therefore we have extracted the standard physical database schema meta-models according to the specific SQL standard. But, the conformance of a vendor database management system with a SQL standard by the rule is not complete. That is the reason why we introduce class of vendor-specific physical database schema meta-models. MOF stack presented in column (1) of Table 1 is specific in relation to the MOF stacks in other columns. SUS in column (1) is at the higher abstraction level then SUSs in other columns. For example, a SUS may be a generic, logical relational database schema of UniversityDb information system (UNIRDBS). This SUS is represented by generic relational database schema meta-model that is conformant with relational data model meta-model. In columns (2), (3) and (4) SUS is the same logical data structure of a database that may be represented by a conceptual database schema, a logical database schema or a database schema based

Table 1 A Classification of Database Meta-Models

MOF level	MOF Architecture				
M3	EMOF/CMOF/Ecore				
M2	Data model meta-model (MM)	Conceptual database schema MM	Implementation database schema MM		Physical dbS MM
			Logical database schema MM	Standard database schema (dbS) MM	Vendor-specific Physical dbS MM
		Generic database schema MM			
	(1)	(2)	(3)	(4)	(5)
	Relational dm MM, OR dm MM, ER dm MM, OO dm MM	ER database schema MM, OO database schema MM,	**Relational database schema MM,** OR database schema MM	SQL:1999 database schema MM, SQL:2003 database schema MM	Oracle 10g database schema MM, MySQL database schema, dBase III+ database schema
M1	ER database schema MM, **Relational database schema MM**, SQL:2003 database schema MM Oracle 10g database schema MM, MySQL database schema	ER database schema 1, ER database schema 2, OO database schema 1, OO database schema 2	Relational database schema of *UniversityDb* IS, Relational database schema 2, OR database schema 1	SQL:2003 database schema 1, SQL:2003 database schema 2, SQL:1999 database schema 1,	Oracle 10g database schema of *UniversityDb* IS, MySQL database schema 1, MySQL database schema 2,
M0	ER database schema 2, Relational database schema of *UniversityDb* IS, SQL:2003 database schema 2, SQL:1999 database schema 1, Oracle10g database schema 1, MySQL database schema	Logical data structure of a database			Database instance

49

	1		

on an SQL standard, respectively. If it is, for example, represented by generic logical relational database schema of *UniversityDb* information system (UNIRDBS), then UNIRDBS is at the M1 level of MOF stack in column (3), while it is at the M0 level of the MOF stack in column (1). SUS in column (5) is a database instance that is represented by an Oracle 10g database schema of *UniversityDb* IS (UNIORA), e.g. UNIORA conforms to Oracle 10g database schema meta-model. The UNIORA2UNIRDBS transformation, which is aimed at transforming of an Oracle 10g physical database schema to a logical, relational database schema, is based on Oracle 10g database schema meta-model and generic relational database schema meta-model. Therefore, these two meta-models are in support of database model transformation UNIORA2UNIRDBS. If the Table 1 is viewed by columns in accordance with the OMG's MDA model classification it can be concluded that:

- Models from column (5) are fully PSM, since they are specific for a platform and its vendor;
- Models from column (4) are PSM, but with the lower level of platform specificity then the models from column (5).
- Models from columns (1) and (3) can be seen as PSM or as PIM depending on platform context UNIRDBS is PSM since it conforms relational data model, but it is PIM since it can represent different vendor specific physical database schemas e.g.; and
- Models from column (2) are PIMs.

Our classification and distribution of database models across the MOF level stack will enable systematic approach for mapping specification between different models/meta-models and development of appropriate M2M or M2T transformations. In order to do that, corresponding meta-models have to be specified. In this paper we are presenting a relational database schema meta-model, according the theoretical definition of relational data model, [12, 15, 21].

3. A Relational Database Schema Meta-Model

Proposed meta-model is fairly huge and complex, so we use packages to organize the meta-model. Modeling concepts in the relational database schema meta-model (RDBSMM) are: attribute, constraint, relation scheme, Universal Relational Schema (URS), relational database schema and project (Fig. 1). In our approach we want to support different database design approaches, and therefore we include URS to support database design approaches based on the URS assumption 21. A database design methodology based on such approach extracts relational database schema from: set of attributes associated with domains, set of functional dependencies and set of non-trivial inclusion dependencies.

A database project is composed from URS and relational database schema. As can be seen in Fig. 2 database constraints may be specialized as: URS constraints, relational constraints and multi-relational constraints. The package representing URS meta-model is presented in Subsection 3.1, and the package representing the relational database schema concept meta-model is presented in Subsection 3.2. In order to make some of the meta-model concepts clearer in Section 4 we give an example of a relation database schema instantiating some of the concepts presented here.

3.1. A URS Meta-Model

Basic constructs of URS meta-model are: attribute and three possible kinds of URS constraints: domain, functional dependency and non-trivial inclusion dependency (see Fig. 3). Domain (*DomainCon*) can be primitive (predefined) domain (*PrimitiveDomain*) or user defined domain (*UserDefDomain*) that can inherit primitive domain (*UserDefDomainFromPrimitiv*) or previously defined user defined domain (*UserDefDomain FromUserDef*). Each attribute is associated with one and only one domain. For a functional dependency (fd) the sets of attributes on the left-hand and right-hand sides of fd are specified. The set of attributes on the right-hand side of the fd may be empty. Unlike fd, both the left-hand and the right-hand side attribute sets of an inclusion dependency (*InclusionDependencyURS*) are non-empty.

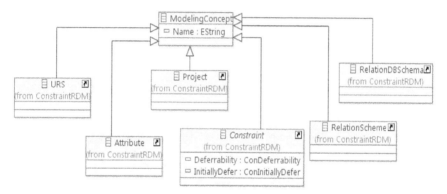

Figure 1: The Relational Database Schema Modeling Concepts

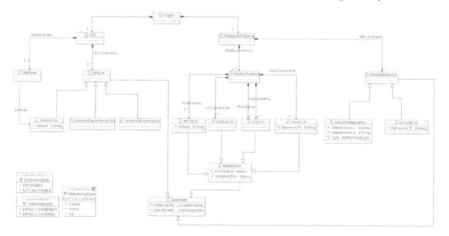

Figure 2 A Meta-Model of Project Concept

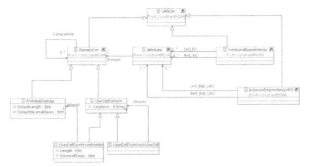

Figure 3. A Meta-Model of URS concept

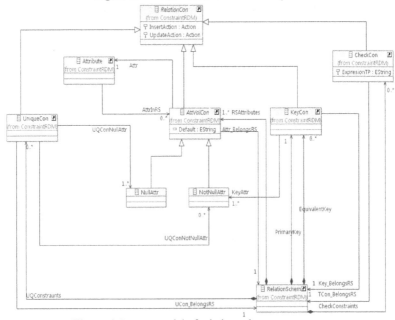

Figure 4.A meta-model of relation scheme concept

3.2. A Meta-Model of Relational Database Schema Concept

A relational database schema is composed of a set of relation schemes and a set of multi-relational constraints (Figure. 4). A relation scheme is composed of a set of attribute value constraints (AttValCon), a set of unique constraints (UniqueCon), a set of key constraints (KeyCon) and a set of check (tuple) constraints (CheckCon) (see Figure. 4). All of these constraints are specializations of relational scheme constraint concept (RelationCon in Figure. 4). In Figure. 5 a meta-model of inclusion dependency (IND) concept (InclusionDependency) is presented. The IND concept may be specialized as key-based IND (referential integrity constraint, RIC, meta-model concept ReferentialIntegrityCon) or as non-key-based IND (NonKeyBasedIND). The non-key-based IND concept is further specialized as inverse referential integrity constraint (IRIC, meta-model concept InverseReferentialIntegrity Con) and as non-IRIC (NonInverseReferential IntegrityCon). Each of RIC, IRIC and non-IRIC concepts may be further specialized as extended RIC (ExReferentialIntegrityCon), extended IRIC (ExInverseReferentialIntegrityCon) and extended non-IRIC (ExNonInverseReferentialIntegrityCon), respectively. Detailed description of RICs and IRICs may be found in 3. In Section 4 may be found some instances of aforementioned IND concept and its specializations. Finally, a meta-model of extended tuple constraint is presented in Figure. 6.

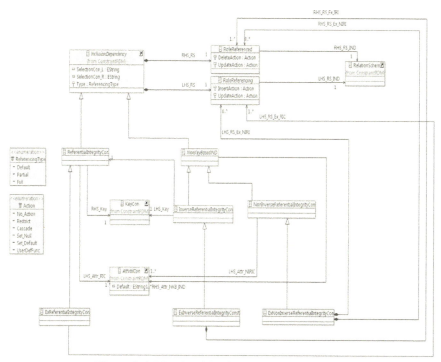

Figure 5. A Meta-Model Of Inclusion Dependency Concept

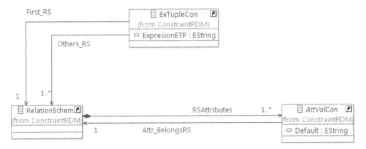

Figure 6. A Meta-Model Of Extended Tuple Constraint Concept

4. An Example of Relational Database Schema

Some kinds of constraints meta-modeled in previous section are well-known and can be implemented by the declarative DBMS mechanisms (like key constraint and RIC). However, some kinds of constraints are not recognized by contemporary DBMSs and have to be implemented through the procedural mechanisms. Very often these kinds of constraints are ignored by database designers in a way that they do not recognize, specify and implement them (like IRIC, selective IND and extended IND). We believe that all kinds of constraints are important to be specified and implemented to achieve the best possible database consistency. That is the reason why we decide to create relational database schema meta-model comprising all kinds of constraints according to theoretically defined relational data model. Here we use the example of University database schema to explain some kinds of constraints that are not broadly accepted within database designers' community. In Figure. 7 the conceptual database schema of University database is visually represented by means of UML class diagram to facilitate better understanding of database constructs and relationships between them. The relational database schema University contains the set of relation schemes: *Employee*, *University*, *Department*, *WorkSite*, *Course*, *EmployedAt* and *Taught_By*, accompanied with the set of multi-relation constraints. A relation scheme is specified as named pair N_L (R_l, C_l), where N_l is the relation scheme name, R_l set of attributes, and C_l set of relation scheme constraints. An inclusion dependency is a statement of the form $N_l[LHS] \subseteq N_r[RHS]$, where *LHS* and *RHS* are non-empty arrays of attributes from R_l and R_r respectively. Having the inclusion operator ($\subseteq$) orientated from the left to right we say that relation scheme N_l is on the left-hand side of the IND, while the relation scheme N_r is on its right-hand side. In the following text we enumerate relation schemes and multi-relation constraints of University database schema and give the explanation of specified constraints.

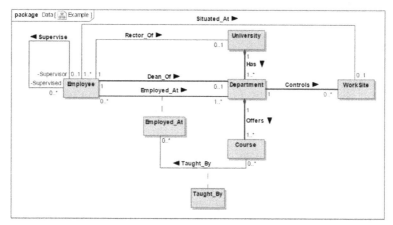

Figure 7. The Conceptual Database Schema of University Database

```
Employee({EmpId, EmpFName, EmpLName, EmpBirthD, EmpSSN,
EmpPosition, PasportNo, SupervisorId, WSId},
{PrimaryKey(EmpId),EquivalentKey(EmpSSN),
Unique(PasportNo),CheckCon((EmpPosition ='Prof' ∨
EmpPosition = 'Assistent') ⇒ WSId IS NOT NULL)})
```

Relation schema *Employee* has two keys (key constraints over the set of attributes) *EmpId* and *EmpSSN*. These constraints are represented by the *KeyCon* concept of RDBSMM (Figure. 4). One of them (*EmpId*) is primary key. The other one is equivalent key. Unique constraint is specified for attribute *PasportNo* since it is nullify attribute in *Employee* and therefore cannot be the part of any key of *Employee*, but if it has value it must be unique within the relation over relation scheme *Employee*. It is represented by the *UniqueCon* concept of RDBSMM (Figure. 4). Specified check constraint models a business rule that University professors and assistants must have worksite (office), while other employees need not. In RDBSMM it is represented by *CheckCon* concept (Figure. 4).

```
University({UniId, UniName, UniCity, RectorId},
{PrimaryKey(UniId)})
Department({UniId, DepId, DepName,
DeanId},{PrimaryKey(UniId+DepId)})WorkSite({WSId, WSLoc,
UniId, DepId}, {PrimaryKey(WSId)})
Course({UniId, DepId, CourseId,
Semester,LectureClassesPW, LabClassesPW}
{PrimaryKey(UniId+DepId+CourseId)})
Employed_At({EmpId, UniId, DepId,
PartTimePct}, {PrimaryKey(EmpId+UniId+DepId)})
Taught_By({UniId,DepId,CourseId,EmpId,
ClassesPerWeek},PrimaryKey(UniId+DepId+CourseId+EmpId)})
```

1. *Employee[SupervisorId]* $\subseteq$ *Employee[EmpId]*
    This is an example of the RIC, since that *EmpId* is an equivalent key of relation scheme *Employee* at the right-hand side of RIC. In RDBSMM it is represented by *ReferentialIntegrityCon* concept (Figure. 5). The RIC is the consequence of URS IND *[SupervisorId]* $\subseteq$ *[EmpId]* that is represented by *InclusionDependecyURS* concept in RDBSMM (Figure. 3).
2. *Employee[WSId]* $\subseteq$ *WorkSite[WSId]*
    This is an example of the RIC, since that *WSId* is the primary key of relation scheme *WorkSite* that is on the right-hand side of the IND.
3. *WorkSite[WSId]* $\subseteq$ *Employee[WSId]*
    The specified constraint is an IRIC, since there is specified RIC (item 2), and *WSId* is the primary key of relation scheme *WorkSite* that is on the left-hand side of the IRIC presented in this item (item 3). In RDBSMM it is represented by *InverseReferentialIntegrityCon* concept (Figure. 5).
4. *University [RectorId]* $\subseteq$ $\sigma_{EmpPosition = \text{'Prof'}}$ *Employee[EmpId]*
    Here we have an example of selective RIC, since there is a selection condition *EmpPosition* = 'Prof' on the right-hand side of IND. The selection condition can be specified using the feature *SelectionCon_R* of *InclusionDependency* concept from the meta-model in Figure. 5. This constraint models a business rule that the rector of the university may be only an employed professor.
5. *Department [UniId]* $\subseteq$ *University [UniId]*(RIC)
6. *University [UniId]* $\subseteq$ *Department[UniId]*(IRIC)
7. *Department [DeanId]* $\subseteq$ $\sigma_{EmpPosition = \text{'Prof'}}$ *Employee [EmpId]*
    This is another selective IND modeling a business rule that the dean of a department may be only an employed professor.
8. *WorkSite [UniId + DepId]* $\subseteq$ *Department[UniId + DepId]* (RIC)
9. *WorkSite* ▷◁ *Employee[EmpId +UniId+DepID+WSid]* $\subseteq$ *Employed_At*▷◁ *Employee [EmpId + UniId + DepId + WSid]*
    Here we have an example of extended non-IRIC. It is extended for the fact that on the one of the IND sides (here on the both of them) there is a join of at least two relations. It is non-IRIC since the array of attributes *EmpId + UniId + DepId + WSid* is not the equivalent key neither for the relation scheme on the left-hand side nor for the relation scheme on the right-hand side of the IND. In RDBSMM it is represented by *ExNonInverseReferentia lIntegrityCon* concept (Figure. 5). The constraint models a business rule that an employee can have only one office and that office has to be located in the worksite that is under control of a department that is one of the departments in which the employee is employed.
10. *Course[UniId + DepId]* $\subseteq$ *Department[UniId + DepId]* (RIC)
11. *Department[UniId + DepId]* $\subseteq$ *Course[UniId + DepId]* (IRIC)
12. *Employed_At[EmpId]* $\subseteq$ *Employee[EmpId]* (RIC)
13. *Employee[EmpId]* $\subseteq$ *Employed_At[EmpId]* (IRIC)
14. *Employed_At[UniId + DepId]* $\subseteq$ *Department[UniId + DepId]* (RIC)
15. *Taught_By[UniId +DepId + CourseId]* $\subseteq$ *Course[UniId + DepId + CourseId]* (RIC)

16. *Taught_By*[*EmpId + UniId + DepId*] $\subseteq$ $\sigma_{EmpPosition = \text{'Prof' or } EmpPosition = \text{'Assistent'}}$
Employed_At▷◁*Employee*[*EmpId+UniI+DepId*]

This is an example of selective extended IND that models businesses rule that only a professor or an assistant that is employed at the department that offers a course may be engaged as a teacher of the course. This constraint is represented by *ExNonInverseReferential IntegrityCon* concept alongside with the feature *SelectionCon_R* of *InclusionDependency* concept of RDBSMM (Figure. 5).

17. ($\forall t \in Employee \triangleright\triangleleft Taught\_By \triangleright\triangleleft Course$)

(((t[*EmpPosition*] = 'Prof' $\Rightarrow$
   t[*ClassesPerWeek*] $<= t$[*LectureClassesPW*]) $\wedge$
(t[*EmpPosition*] = 'Assistent' $\Rightarrow$
   t[*ClassesPerWeek*] $<= t$[*LabClassesPW*]))

Here is an example of extended tuple constraint. It is extended since it mutually constraints values of the attributes from different relations, but it is tuple constraint since these values are from only one tuple that belongs to a join of at least two relations. In RDBSMM it is represented by *ExTupleCon* concept (Figure. 6). This constraint models the business rule that a professor may teach only lecture classes, and therefore, classes per week that he/she has for that course has to be less or equal than the number of lecture classes for the course per week. Besides, an assistant may teach only laboratory classes, and therefore, classes per week that he/she has for that course has to be less or equal than the number of laboratory classes for the course per week.

5. Related Work

Mapping of object/OR/ER/EER models to relational database schemas and vice versa has been widely used as a case study to present new model transformations proposals. Atzeni, Cappellari and Gianforme in [1] propose a framework focused on schema mappings. The proposal is based on a relational database formal basis, but the usage of a new meta-meta-model (known-as Supermodel), different from MOF, makes it hard to develop bridges towards the universe of MOF-compliant proposals. The importance of generic models is also emphasized by Atzeni, Gianforme and Cappellari in [2]. They have shown how a meta-model approach can be the basis for numerous model-generic and model-aware techniques. A dictionary to store their schemas and models, a specific supermodel (a data model that generalizes all models of interest) is presented, too. They presented a classification of data model constructs and their distribution beyond six data models.

Gogolla et al. in [17] have sketched how syntax and semantics of the ER and relational data model and their transformation can be understood as platform independent and platform specific models. Presented ER and relational meta-models are very simple and cannot be classified according meta-model classification presented in our work. This paper is interesting in another context: it presents the intensional and extensional ER/relational meta-models. The relational database schema meta-model that we presented in this paper is an intensional meta-model. Our future research has to consider extensional database meta-models, too. Polo,

Garcia-Rodriguez and Piattini in [23] present the technical and functional descriptions of a tool specifically designed for database re-engineering. In the case study they propose simplified relational and object-oriented meta-model. Both of them are too simple to be classified according to meta-model classification presented in our paper.

The similar, simplified RDBMS meta-model is presented in [28], where Wang, Shen and Chen emphasize that the assumption that the DDL statements can be extracted easily through DBMS is not always true. In paper [27], the authors propose through a case study supported by a tool, a model-driven development of OR database schemas. To that end, Vara et al. have implemented an ATL model transformation that generates an OR database model from a conceptual data model and a MOFScript model to text transformation that generates the SQL code for the modeled database schema. As part of the proposal they have defined a MOF-based Domain Specific Language (DSL) for OR database modeling as well as a graphical editor for such DSL. They presented Oracle 10g meta-model that can be classified as vendor-specific physical database schema meta-model according to the classification presented in our paper. Lano and Kolahdouz-Rahimi in [18] and [19] presented case study of UML to relational database model transformation. In the context of relational database schema meta-model presented in our paper the relational database meta-model presented in [18] and [19] is rather simplified and does not differentiate between standard and vendor specific constructs. In [11] a process is proposed to automatically generate Web Services from relational databases. SQL-92 meta-model has been used to represent the database model, that can be classified as standard physical database schema meta-model according to the classification presented in our paper.

Calero et al. in [10] have introduced ontology for increasing the understandability of the SQL2003 concepts. Their SQL: 2003 meta-model can be seen as a standard database schema meta-model. Cabot and Teniente in [9] presents an OCL meta-model that defines a set of techniques and a method of their integration, for the efficient checking of OCL integrity constraints specified in a UML conceptual schema. Cabot et al. in [8] present a new method for the analysis of declarative M2M transformations based on the automatic extraction of OCL invariants implicit in the transformation definition. In a case study, they used simplified UML class meta-model, that can be classified as a generic database schema meta-model according to the classification presented in our paper.

Guerra et al. in [16] stress that model transformations should be engineered, not hacked. For this purpose, they have presented transML, a family of languages to help building transformations using well-founded engineering principles. They presented platform meta-model, meta-model of the specification languages and mapping meta-model. They are not in the direct correlation with the results presented in our paper, but may be interesting in our further research of the database re-engineering process.

In the paper [13] Eessaar explained why it is advantageous to create meta-model of a data model. He demonstrated that a meta-model could be used in order to find similarities and differences with other data models. Beggar, Bousetta and Gadi [6] propose a reverse engineering process based on MDSE that presents a solution to provide a normalized relational database which includes the integrity constraints extracted from legacy data. They extract entirely the description of legacy data from only source code and physical files. COBOL file section meta-model is proposed, that can be classified as generic file schema meta-model.

6. Conclusion

The value of models and abstractions in software development is substantial in order to master system complexity. MDSE has become a commonly used approach in software engineering. It promotes using models as primary artifacts and proposes methods for transforming them to desired software products. Model transformations are defined in order to bridge different modeling languages or to map between representations in the same language. Complex data mapping tasks often arise in MDSE. A number of data models are in common use and each data model provides slightly different modeling structures.

One important advantage of having multiple data models is that developers can select the data model that offers the most convenient representation for their particular needs. However, the use of multiple data models introduces the possibility of many kinds of structural heterogeneity. Therefore, the transformations between different database models are very important. That was our motivation to focus on database models and meta-models they are conformant with. Meta-modeling is widely spread area of research and there is a huge number of references covering MOF based meta-models. It is easy to conclude, based on the literature review in the previous section, that a lot of authors use or propose different database meta-models. However, to the best of our knowledge, we could not find any systematical overview of database meta-models at different abstraction levels.

The main contribution of our paper may be two folded: through the database meta-model classification presented in Section 2 and through detailed relational database schema meta-model, as proposed in Section 3. We believe that both contributions will enable our future efforts directed towards automating database and information system re-engineering process based on MDSE principles. We have used presented meta-model of relational database schema to develop a chain of M2M transformations starting with a legacy relational database schema and to integrate them with our IIS*Studio development environment 3. The chain of these transformations enables reverse engineering, while IIS*Studio tool is used for forward engineering and generating executable application prototypes. Category theory [24], [25] provides a kind of common language and tool, in which a sketch is a specification based on graphs as the formal structure. We plan to investigate a possible usage of category theory for PIM specification of model transformations in order to automate the process of database model transformations generation.

Summary

Model-Driven Software Engineering (MDSE) aims to provide automated support for the development, maintenance and evolution of software by performing transformations on models. During these transformations model elements are traced from a more abstract model to a more concrete model and vice versa, achieved through meta-modeling. Software development process produces numerous models of complex application artifacts, such as application programs, databases, web sites or user interfaces. In the paper we focus on models related to databases. For these models we use a generic name database models. They may be created at several, usually different levels of abstraction. In order to specify and generate model transformations between these database models, theirs meta-models have to be defined. In the paper, we propose a classification of database models and meta-models that are involved in the database model transformations. Also, we present a meta-model of relational database schema specified by means of the Eclipse Modeling Framework (EMF) and based on the EMF Ecore meta-meta-model which is closely aligned with the Essential MOF (EMOF) specification.

References

1. P. Atzeni, P. Cappellari, and G. Gianforme: MIDST: model independent schema and data translation. In Proceedings of the 2007 ACM SIGMOD international Conference on Management of Data (Beijing, China, June 11 - 14, 2007). SIGMOD '07. ACM, New York, NY, 1134-1136 (2007).

2. P. Atzeni, G. Gianforme, P. Cappellari: A universal meta-model and its dictionary. T. Large-Scale Data and Knowledge-Centered Systems 1, 38–62 (2009).

3. S. Aleksic, S. Ristic, I. Lukovic, M. Celikovic A Design Specification and a Server Implementation of the Inverse Referential Integrity Constraints. ComSIS, Consortium of Faculties of Serbia and Montenegro, Belgrade, Serbia, ISSN: 1820-0214, Vol. 10, No. 1, 283-320 (2013).

4. U. Assmann, S. Zchaler, G. Wagner: Ontologies, Meta-Models, and the Model-Driven Paradigm. In: Calero, C., Ruiz, F., Piattini, M. (eds.) Ontologies for Software Engineering and Software Technology (2006).

5. C. Atkinson, T. Kuhne: A Generalized Notion of Platforms for Model-Driven Development, In Model-Driven Software Development, ed. Sami Beydeda, Matthias Book and Volker Gruhn, Berlin Heidelberg: Springer, 119–136 (2005).

6. O. El Beggar, B. Bousetta, and T. Gadi, "Getting Relational Database from Legacy Data-MDRE Approach", Computer Engineering and Intelligent Systems www.iiste.org ISSN 2222-1719 (Paper) ISSN 2222-2863 (Online) Vol 4, No.4, (2013).

7. P. Bernstein: Applying Model Management to Classical Meta Data Problems. Paper presented at the Conference on Innovative Database Research (CIDR), Asilomar, CA, (2003).

8. J. Cabot, R. Clarisó, E. Guerra, J. De Lara: Verification and validation of declarative model-to-model transformations through invariants. Journal of Systems and Software, 83(2), 283-302 (2010).

9. J. Cabot, E. Teniente: Incremental integrity checking of uml/ocl conceptual

schemas. Journal of Systems and Software, 82(9), 1459–1478 (2009).

10. C. Calero, F. Ruiz, A. Baroni, E. Brito, F. Abreu, M. Piattini: An ontological approach to describe the SQL:2003 object-relational features. Computer Standards & Interfaces, Volume 28, Issue 6, September 2006, Pages 695–713 (2006).

11. R. P. del Castillo, I. García-Rodríguez, I. Caballero: PRECISO: a reengineering process and a tool for database modernization through web services. In: Jacobson Jr., M.J., Rijmen, V., Safavi-Naini, R. (eds.) SAC 2009. LNCS, vol. 5867, pp. 2126–2133 (2009).

12. C. J. Date, H. Darwen: Types and the Relational Model. The Third Manifesto, 3rd ed. Addison Wesley, (2006).

13. E. Eessaar: Using Meta-modeling in order to Evaluate Data Models. In Proceedings of the 6th WSEAS Int. Conf. on Artificial Intelligence, Knowledge Engineering and Data Bases, Corfu Island, Greece, February 16-19, (2007).

14. Eclipse Modeling Framework, [Online] Available: http://www.eclipse.org/modeling/emf/. (retrieved January, 05, 2013).

15. R. Elmasri, and B. S. Navathe, Database Systems: Models, Languages, Design and Application Programming, Sixth Edition, Pearson Global Edition, ISBN 978-0-13-214498-8. (2011).

16. E. Guerra, J. de Lara, D. Kolovos, R. Paige, O. dos Santos: Engineering model transformations with transML. Software and Systems Modeling. Springer-Verlag, (2011).

17. M. Gogolla, A. Lindow, M. Richters, P. Ziemann: Meta-model transformation of data models. Position paper. WISME at the UML (2002).

18. K. Lano, S. Kolahdouz-Rahimi: Model-driven development of model transformations. Theory and Practice of Model Transformations, 47-61 (2011).

19. K. Lano, S. Kolahdouz-Rahimi: Constraint-based specification of model transformations Journal of Systems and Software, Volume 86, Issue 2, Pages 412–436 (2013).

20. Meta-Object Facility, [Online] Available: http://www.omg.org/mof/. (retrieved January, 05, 2013).

21. P. Mogin, I. Luković, M. Govedarica: Database Design Principles, University of Novi Sad, Faculty of Technical Sciences & MP "Stylos", Novi Sad, Serbia, (2004).

22. J. Mukerji, J. Miller: MDA Guide Version 1.0.1, document omg/03-06-01 (MDA Guide V1.0.1), http://www.omg.org/, (retrieved January, 05, 2013).

23. M. Polo, I. Garcia-Rodriguez, M. Piattini: An MDA-based approach for database re-engineering. J. Softw. Maint. Evol. 19, 6, 383-417 (2007).

24. V. Slodičák V.: Some useful structures for categorical approach for program behavior, Journal of Information and Organizational Sciences, Vol. 35, No. 1, pp. 99-109, 1846-9418, www.jos.foi.hr (2011).

25. C. Szabó, V. Slodičák: Software Engineering Tasks Instrumentation by Category Theory, SAMI 2011, Proceedings of the 9th IEEE International Symposium on Applied Machine Intelligence and Informatics, Smolenice, Slovakia, 2011, Košice, elfa, s.r.o., pp. 195-199. (2011).

26. T. Stahl, M. Völter, J. Bettin, A. Haase, S. Helsen: Model Driven Software

Development: Technology, Engineering, Management. John Wiley & Sons, Ltd, (2006).

27. J. Vara, B. Vela, V. A. Bollati, E. Marcos: Supporting model-driven development of object-relational database schemas: a case study, in: R. Paige (Ed.), Theory and Practice of Model Transformations, Heidelberg, Springer Berlin, pp. 181–196 (2009).

28. H. Wang, B. Shen, C. Chen: Model-Driven Reengineering of Database. Software Engineering, 2009. WCSE '09. WRI World Congress on , vol.3, no., pp.113-117 (2009).

Chapter 5

Two Study Findings in South Africa of the Technology Acceptance Model: A Comparative Analysis

1. Introduction

Models for information technology (IT) adoption build on theories of behavioural change and attempt to better understand what motivates and influences the adoption of technologies. One popular technology is an Executive Information System (EIS). An EIS is a computerised IS designed to provide managers in organisations with access to internal and external information that is relevant to management activities and decision making. The importance of information for decision-making by executives and managers in organisations has been extensively documented. Without the provision of concise and timely information ([32], [45]), executives will not be able to determine whether their views of the environment and their organisation's position within it, remain appropriate [39]. To benefit from information systems (IS) in decision-making, an increasing number of organisations are implementing IS for direct use by executives and managers, in order to access information, both internally and externally to the organisation. Nowadays, pervasive computing embeds computing and (IT) into organisational environments, by integrating them seamlessly into the everyday lives of executives and managers, in order to augment decision-making support. It is evident that the adoption and implementation of IT and IS in organisations is an important consideration for both practitioners and researchers in the field. Cabral, Lucas & Gordon [14], indicate that there have been few empirical studies of technology adoption models in developing country settings. South Africa is a developing country. EIS are found in many organisations in South Africa [8].

2. Research Environment

User acceptance of IT has been a primary focus in IT implementation research for the past two decades - where IT adoption and use has been a major goal of organisations. Researchers in the field rely on the theories of innovation diffusion to study implementation problems [4]. Davis states that in TAM, perceived usefulness and perceived ease of use are the two factors that govern the adoption and use of IT [20]. TAM has strong behavioural elements and assumes that when someone forms an intention to act, that they will be free to act without limitation. TAM is one of the dominant research models which have been widely used [18]. However, research in Africa using TAM is limited [44]. This study will therefore contribute towards a better understanding of the Perceived Usefulness (PU) and Perceived Ease of Use (PEOU) constructs related to TAM in Africa (in a selected area of South Africa). The purpose of this article is to analyse the PU and PEOU constructs during EIS development and implementation in organisations in the eThekwini Municipal Area (EMA), KwaZulu-Natal, South Africa. The article focuses on the findings of two selected TAM/EIS studies in the EMA:

- A survey of 31 organisations conducted by Udo Richard Averweg, which is reported in Averweg [7] and hereafter referred to as the 'Averweg (2002) study.
- A case study conducted at Unilever South Africa (Pty) Ltd (Head Office, Umhlanga Ridge) by Sonny Anyetei Moses Ako-Nai [3], which is hereafter referred to as the 'Ako-Nai (2005) study'.

Since this article focuses on the summarised results of these two studies, it should be noted that the research approaches adopted in the Averweg (2002) study and the Ako-Nai (2005) study, are not compared.

3. Information Systems Adoption and Use

User acceptance and continuous usage (adoption) are important determinants in gauging success or failure of an IS. Computer or IS usage has been identified as the key indicator of the adoption of IT by organisations [38]. Igbaria & Tan [27] report that system usage is an important variable in IT acceptance, as it appears to be a good surrogate measure for the effective deployment of IS resources in organisations. User acceptance factors have been a long-standing research issue [3]. Clearly, IS adoption and use is an important topic in scholarly discourse.

Since EIS are classified as high-risk projects, organisations are cautious and critical in dealing with them, in order to ensure successful EIS implementation and continuous usage by executives - the intended users [9]. An organisation seeks to avoid failure of its newly implemented EIS, and proactively wants to identify possible factors relating to users' attitudes towards the IS. These factors are likely to influence (positively or negatively) the IS users' acceptance, adoption and use of the system. Lu & Gustafson [33] report that people use computers because they believe they will increase their problem-solving performance (usefulness), and are relatively easy to use. These researchers suggest that the two belief variables, PU and PEOU, are the most important factors determining usage of computers or IS.

4. Technology Acceptance Model

TAM was developed by Davis [20] and postulates that two particular beliefs - PU and PEOU are of primary relevance for computer acceptance behaviors ([22], [28], and [31]). According to TAM, system use is determined by a person's attitude towards the system (see Figure 1). The basic TAM model consists of external variables which may affect beliefs. The model is derived from the general Theory of Reasoned Action (TRA) [24], in that TAM is intended to explain computer use. In IT terms, this means that the model attempts to explain the attitude towards using IT, rather than the attitude towards IT itself. According to Chooprayoon & Fung

[18], TAM has been "verified and confirmed by many scholars as a practical theoretical model for the investigation of users' behaviour". Furthermore, according to Singh, Singh, Singh & Singh [36], TAM has examined the attitude and belief of users - that influences their acceptance or rejection of using IT. TAM has the advantage of 'first mover advantage', as one of the early IS theories. The TAM model of IS success relies on the TRA of Fishbein & Ajzen [24] and Ajzen & Fishbein [2] - to assert that two factors are primary determinants of system use:

- Perceived Usefulness (PU). PU is defined as the user's subjective probability that using a specific technology will increase his or her job performance, within an organisational setting [22]; and
- Perceived Ease of Use (PEOU). PEOU is the end-user's assessment that the IS will be easy to use and requires little effort.

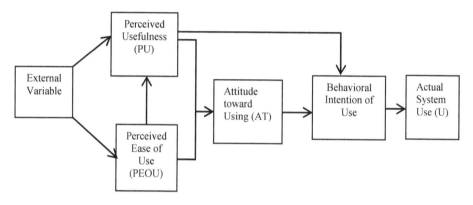

Figure 1. Technology Acceptance Model [22]

Davis' model specifically postulates that technology use is determined by behavioural intention to use the technology; which is itself determined by both PU and PEOU. TAM identified PU as the single largest contributor towards Behavioural Intention of Use (BI), while PEOU exerts a strong influence on PU but a weaker direct influence on BI [20]. Studies have shown that both PU and PEOU have positive effects on U and BI [35]. TAM-related studies have confirmed that PU is generally a much stronger predictor of perceived intent to use than PEOU [34]. BI acts as a mediator between other variables which exert their influence on U through this variable [44]. Research findings suggest that TAM measures appear to be relatively free of measurement biases and also serve as a robust model from both a theoretical and measurement perspective [21]. During the Averweg (2002) study and Ako-Nai (2005) study, the PU and PEOU constructs were operationalised by obtaining end-users' assessment of their PU and PEOU of EIS.

Straub, Keil & Brenner [37] suggest that PU of computers has a positive effect on the adoption of IT. Jeyaraj, Rottman & Lacity [30] report that they "did not find good support for a direct relationship between *Ease of Use* and IT adoption, there is ample evidence of a direct relationship between *Perceived Usefulness* and IT adoption". Adams, Nelson & Todd [1] and Connelly [19] report that PU affects both attitudes and actual computer use. Hu, Chau, Liu Sheng & Yan Tam [26] suggest that PU is a significant determinant of attitude and intention, while Brown [26] reports that PU is not a significant influence on use. Later research by Bagozzi [10] questioned the possibility of determining behaviour by adding up measures for PU and PEOU. He considered that there may be differential contributions of salient beliefs. Bagozzi concluded that the TAM model may not be suitable for explaining and predicting system use.

Burton-Jones & Hubona [13] replicated TAM with a survey of 125 employees in a United States of America government agency. Information regarding respondents' beliefs and usage behaviour were collated and analysed. The results showed that PU and PEOU may not mediate all influences from external environmental factors on systems usage. Burton-Jones & Hubona [13] suggested that some external actors (e.g. system experience, level of education, age) may have a direct effect on system use. TAM has also been challenged as an appropriate model for developing countries and IS adoption [5]. TAM has been widely accepted and applied in a variety of settings due to its parsimony and exploratory power [15]. The most commonly investigated variables of TAM are PU and PEOU ([20], [[22], [41], [42], [25], [43], [29], [30], [11], [19], [17], [16], and [18]). Jeyaraj et al. [30] suggest that the high utilisation of PU and PEOU shows the dominance of TAM in individual adoption research, and they state that the constructs have been used in the literature more than twice as often as other constructs.

Chang et al. [26] indicate that the TAM literature "has a steady growth as well as the citations". However, Chuttur [17] suggests that although TAM is a highly cited model, researchers share mixed opinions regarding its theoretical assumptions and practical effectiveness. Nevertheless, Hendriks & Jacobs [25] argue that TAM's popularity derives from its common sense nature, simplicity and robustness. The literature review suggests that TAM is the most widely used model to predict technology acceptance and, by implication, use [44]. This serves as the rationale for exploring the PU and PEOU constructs in this article.

5. Discussion of Two Selected TAM/EIS Studies

A discussion of the PU and PEOU constructs of TAM/EIS in the Averweg (2002) study and Ako-Nai (2005) study is now given.

5.1. Averweg (2002) Study

The Spearman rank-order correlation coefficients r were calculated for PU and AT; and PEOU and AT. Averweg [7] reported that after allowing for tied observations, $r = 0.144$ for PU and $r = 0.373$ for PEOU. These correlation values were considerably lower than expected. For example, Davis [20] reports "Perceived usefulness was correlated .63 with self-reported current use in Study 1 and .85 with self-predicted use in Study 2. Perceived ease of use was correlated .45 with use in Study 1 and .69 in Study 2". Averweg's correlation [7] for usefulness-use ($r = 0.144$) was *lower* than for ease of use-use ($r = 0.373$) and was therefore not consistent with Davis' findings. Furthermore, Averweg reported low correlation values and PU was *not* "significantly more strongly linked to usage than was ease of use" [20]. Davis [20] emphasised that PU and PEOU are people's subjective appraisal of performance and effort, respectively, and do not necessarily reflect objective reality.

5.2. Ako-Nai (2005) Study

The Spearman rank-order correlation coefficients r were calculated for PU and AT; and PEOU and AT. They are reflected in Table 1 (below).

Table 1: Spearman rank-order correlation coefficients [3]

R	Before adjustment	After adjustment
Between PU and AT	0.238	0.238
Between PEOU and AT	0.340	0.459

Ako-Nai [3] reported that the positive correlation coefficients between the variables PU, PEU and AT indicated a relationship between them (as postulated by TAM) and the strength of the relationship is measured by the indicated values (Freund *et al.*, 1993 cited in [3]). However, these values were low and this can be attributed to the low heterogeneous nature of the data results obtained. Ako-Nai reported that following an inspection of the raw data, there were very low variations in response (mostly in the range '5 slightly agree and 7 strongly agree). Ako-Nai further indicated that a similar result was obtained and highlighted in the Averweg (2002) study. Ako-Nai suggested that a positive but low correlation coefficient can also be attributed to the fact that the EIS at Unilever South Africa (Pty) Ltd is still at its earliest stage of diffusion in the organisation.

Ako-Nai indicated that it was his expectation (and in accordance with the TAM model) that the influence of PU on AT should be greater than that of PEOU on AT. However, the researcher experienced "surprise findings or a lack of expected findings" as there "was the reverse impact values of the two factors, PU and PEU, on AT" [3]. Ako-Nai found that the correlation factor of PEU on AT was higher (both before and after adjustments) than of PU – which is a contradiction of the expectations from the TAM postulated construct.

6. Summary of Two Selected TAM/EIS Studies

A summary for each of the findings from the Averweg (2002) study and the Ako-Nai (2005) study is now presented.

6.1. Averweg (2002) Study

The Averweg [7] study finding was that PEOU on intended use was greater than the effect of PU on intended use. As the researcher reported low correlation values, an investigation was made by him of the raw data. It was found that if a correlation coefficient is based on only three (out of seven possible different Likert-type scale categories), there is potential for a problem. For higher correlations, greater variation is required from respondents regarding their intended EIS use. In previous findings (see, for example, [4], [38]) significantly higher correlation results were reported. Averweg [7] reported that while the low correlation results may be disappointing, this may be ascribed to the fact there were very small statistical variations in interviewee's responses.

While the Averweg (2002) study was limited to existing EIS in organisations in the EMA, the researcher felt that due to the similarities between the economy in KwaZulu Natal and the rest of South Africa, the results can be considered as an approximate indicator for the South African economy. This means that although the researcher's results were limited, they do provide a meaningful reflection of EIS adoption in the EMA. The researcher concluded that in the Averweg (2002) study there was little evidence to support that the theoretical use aspects of TAM were echoed in EIS implementation in KwaZulu-Natal.

6.2. Ako-Nai (2005) Study

Ako-Nai [3] reported that high emphasis on PEOU was recorded given respondent's comments on the flexibility of the EIS when compared to previous SAP/BW systems. According to these respondents, such previous IS lacked flexibility, were complex to use and were not user-friendly. On the other hand, since the EIS was more flexible and easy-to-use, the respondents responded positively.

PU scored a high mean value of 5.46. All the contributing factors to PU had mean score values above 5 ('slightly agree') except 'I can still do my work without EIS' and 'EIS provides me with all the information I need' factors. These two factors scored mean values of 4.21 and 3.93 respectively. The mean score value for the 'I can still do my work without EIS' factor suggested that end-users were still able to work and utilize other sources of information. The mean score value for the 'EIS provides me with all the information I need' factor suggested that end-users required additional information that was not available in the EIS. This was triangulated with the fact that respondents confirmed other sources of information: internal information (from other systems and SAP/BW) and external information (from Nielson database sources and customer information from customers). Ako-Nai [3] suggested that this finding may also be a contributing factor to the lower influence of PU on AT (when compared to PEOU on AT) and thereby weakened the perceived useful of EIS. The lower influence of PU was further supported when the respondents were asked whether they would continue to function effectively without EIS. While the respondents responded positively, they stated that it would be 'incredibly' difficult and some complexity will be experienced in obtaining all the information required to make decisions.

The researcher in the Ako-Nai (2005) study concluded that for the respondents surveyed, the factors for PEOU and PU had a positive influence on respondents' attitude towards the EIS. The study results also highlighted that PEOU (when compared to PU) has a greater effect on end users' attitude towards using the EIS.

7. Summary of the Two TAM/EIS Studies

User acceptance of technology remains an important field of study in the IS discipline. While many models have been proposed to explain and predict the use of a system, TAM has been *the* model which has captured much attention of the IS community. Despite its frequent use, TAM has been widely criticised and original proponents have attempted to redefine it several times. Attempts by researchers to expand TAM in order to adapt it to constantly changing IT environments has led to "a state of theoretical chaos and confusion" [11].

The Averweg (2002) study and Ako-Nai (2005) study do not support the basic tenets of TAM. TAM has emphasised the importance of PU (over PEOU), as the key determinant of IT acceptance. Empirical evidence has constantly borne out this claim, leading to PEOU being treated as something of a 'step-child' [40]. However, results of Venkatesh's research indicate that PEOU *can* be a strong catalyst fostering IT acceptance. Both the Averweg (2002) study and the Ako-Nai (2005) study partially support this finding, i.e. PEOU can be a stronger catalyst (over PU), in terms of fostering IT acceptance.

The Averweg (2002) study and the Ako-Nai (2005) study both support Brown's findings [12] that "perceived ease of use takes on increased importance, as it influences both usage and perceived usefulness". Doll, Hendrickson & Deng [23] indicate that despite TAM's wide acceptance, a series of incremental cross-validation studies have produced conflicting and equivocal results that do not provide guidance for researchers or practitioners who might use TAM for decision-making purposes. One possible explanation for this is that human memory may not work in the same way that salient beliefs are processed in TAM. This may result in that the intention to use the EIS may not be representative enough of actual use – the time period between intention and adoption can be mitigated by decision-making uncertainties which may influence an individual's decision to adopt and use an IT. In a developing country in Africa, the conventional wisdom that PU is the main predictor of adoption has been challenged [6]. It appears that application of the TAM model to IS (such as an EIS) in developing countries should be guided more by the specificities of local circumstances than by the performance of the TAM model in developed countries. In summary then, the Ako-Nai (2005) study findings corroborated the earlier findings of the Averweg (2002) study. The four major findings (from *both* studies) are now summarised:

- Low correlation coefficients were calculated for the PU-AT and PEOU-AT constructs;
- The correlation for perceived usefulness-use was *lower* than for perceived ease of use-use, which is not consistent with Davis' findings;
- The results *partially* support Venkatesh's findings [40] that PEOU can be a stronger catalyst (over PU) in fostering IT acceptance; and
- There is support for Brown's findings [12] - wherein the TAM PEOU-AT relationship was higher than PU-AT.

8. Conclusion

This study sets out to improve a better understanding of the determinants of use and usefulness to facilitate influencing future EIS implementations. The approach was organizational-specific as it focused on EIS use and the perception of EIS-users, rather than on extraneous factors such as barriers to IT acceptance and possible changes in the IT environment of organizations. Since the Averweg (2002) study and Ako Nai (2005) study were conducted, pervasive computing has resulted in a move away from "the traditional desktop model of computing towards having technology embedded in the environment" [19]. Future research may therefore need to be directed to investigating the role of other potential antecedents, in order to enhance IT adoption and assimilation variances in the EMA. It is acknowledged that this study was limited by its relatively narrow geographical and institutional focus in the EMA. However, this limitation may open up opportunities for future research. For example, qualitative research can contribute to enhancing and deepening the understanding of practitioner practices that drive the implementation and adoption of EIS in organizations.

While it may be tempting to conclude that research on TAM may have reached a saturation level, future research should focus on developing new models that will exploit the strengths of the TAM model while discarding its weaknesses [17]. One suggestion in this regard, is investigating the specificities of local developing country circumstances, the facilitating conditions (e.g. socio-economic status) and the individual difference variables (such as experience, level of education, age, gender) to increase the final IT use prediction of EIS (in organizations in the EMA). Furthermore, general pervasive computing conditions in organizations in South Africa may serve as an appealing context in which to investigate IT adoption. Possible extensions to TAM should also be considered. Such IT acceptance studies should pay attention to issues of significance in assessing the contributions of variables explaining IT usage for decision making by executives and managers in these organizations.

Summary

Models for information technology (IT) adoption build on theories of behavioral change and attempt to better understand what motivates and influences the adoption of technologies. One popular technology is an Executive Information System (EIS). An EIS is a computerized information system, designed to provide managers in organizations with access to internal and external information that is relevant to management activities and decision-making. IT acceptance studies pay much attention to issues of significance in assessing the contributions of variables explaining IT usage for decision-making in organizations. Davis' Technology Acceptance Model (TAM) states that Perceived Usefulness (PU) and Perceived Ease of Use (PEOU) are the two factors that govern the adoption and use of IT. In this article, discussion is made of the findings of two TAM/EIS studies in the eThekwini Municipal Area (EMA), KwaZulu-Natal, South Africa. From these

TAM/EIS studies, are four findings: (1) low correlation coefficients were calculated for the PU-AT and PEOU-AT constructs; (2) the correlation for perceived usefulness-use was lower than for perceived ease of use-use, which is not consistent with Davis' findings; (3) the results partially support Venkatesh's findings [40] that PEOU can be a stronger catalyst (over PU) in fostering IT acceptance; and (4) there is support for Brown's findings [12] - wherein the TAM PEOU-AT relationship was higher than PU-AT.

References

1. Adams, D.A., Nelson, R.R. & Todd, P.A. Perceived usefulness, ease of use, and usage of Information Technology: A replication, MIS Quarterly, 16(2): 227-247 (1992).
2. Ajzen, I. & Fishbein, M.: 1980. Understanding attitudes and predicting social behavior. Englewood Cliffs, New Jersey: Prentice-Hall (1980).
3. Ako-Nai, S.A.M.: Executive Information Systems: An identification of factors likely to affect user acceptance, usage and adoption of the Unilever EIS. Master of Business Administration dissertation, Faculty of Management, University of KwaZulu-Natal, Durban, South Africa (2005).
4. Al-Gahtani, S.S.: The applicability of the Technology Acceptance Model outside North America: An empirical test in the Arab world, BITWorld 2001 Conference Proceedings, American University in Cairo, Egypt, June 4-6 (2001).
5. Anandarajan, M., Igbaria, M. & Anakwe, U.P.: Technology acceptance in the Banking Industry: A perspective from a less developed country, Information Technology & People, 13: 298-312 (2000).
6. Anandarajan, M., Igbaria, M. & Anakwe, U.P. IT Acceptance in a less-developed country: A motivational factor perspective, International Journal of Information Management, 22(1): 47-65 (2002).
7. Averweg, U.R.: Information Technology acceptance in South Africa: An investigation of Perceived Usefulness, Perceived Ease of Use, and Actual Use constructs, The African Journal of Information Systems, 1(1): 44-66 (2008).
8. Averweg, U.R.: An account of Executive Information Systems research in South Africa. In M Khosrow Pour (ed) Encyclopedia of Information Science and Technology. Third Edition, IGI Global, Hershey, PA, USA. Forthcoming (2014).
9. Belcher, L.W. & Watson, H.J.: Assessing the value of CONOCO's EIS, MIS Quarterly, 17(4): 239-253 (1993).
10. Bagozzi, R.P.: The legacy of the technology acceptance model and a proposal for a paradigm shift, Journal of the Association for Information Systems, 8(4): 244-254 (2007).
11. Benbasat, I. & Barki, H.: Quo Vadis, TAM? Journal of the Association of Information Systems, 8(4): 211-218 (2007).
12. Brown, I.: Individual and technological factors affecting Perceived Ease of Use of web-based learning technologies in a developing country, The Electronic Journal on Information Systems in Developing Countries, 9(5): 1-15 (2002).

13. Burton-Jones, A. & Hubona, G.S.: The mediation of external variables in the technology acceptance model, Information & Management, 43(6): 706-717 (2006).
14. Cabral, C., Lucas, P. & Gordon, D.: Technology adoption in developing country contexts: testing water for microbial contamination, Aquatest Working Paper No. 03, Aquatest 2 project, Water and Health Research center, Department of Civil Engineering, University of Bristol, United Kingdom, September (2009).
15. Calantone, R.J., Griffith, D.A. & Yalcinkaya, G.: An Empirical Examination of a Technology Adoption Model for the Context of China, Journal of International Marketing, 21(2): 39-61 (2006).
16. Chang, S-H., Chou, C-H. & Yang, J-M.: The literature review of Technology Acceptance Model: A study of the bibliometric distributions, PACIS 201 Proceedings, Available online at: http://aisel.aisnet.org/pacis2010/158 [Accessed 1 November 2012] (2010).
17. Chuttur, M.Y.: Overview of the Technology Acceptance Model: Origins, Developments and Future Directions, Sprouts: Working Papers on Information Systems, 9(37), Indiana University, USA. [Accessed 15 December 2011] (2009).
18. Chooprayoon, V. & Fung, C.C.: TECTAM: An approach to study Technology Acceptance Model (TAM) in gaining knowledge on the adoption and use of e-commerce/e-business technology among small and medium enterprises in Thailand. eCommerce, Kyeong Kang (Ed.) InTech, 31-38 (2010).
19. Connelly, K.: On developing a Technology Acceptance Model for pervasive computing, Proceedings of Ubiquitous System Evaluation (USE) – a workshop at the Ninth International Conference on Ubiquitous Computing (UBICOMP), September (2007).
20. Davis, F.D.: Perceived Usefulness, Perceived Ease of Use, and User Acceptance of Information Technology, MIS Quarterly, 3(3): 319-342 (1989).
21. Davis, F.D. & Venkatesh, V.: A critical assessment of potential measurement biases in the technology acceptance model: three experiments, International Journal of Human-Computer Studies, 45(1): 19-45 (1996).
22. Davis, F.D., Bagozzi, R.P. & Warshaw, P.R.: User Acceptance of computer technology: A comparison of two theoretical models, Management Science, 35(8): 982-1003 (1989).
23. Doll, W.J., Hendrickson, A. & Deng, X.: Using Davis's Perceived Usefulness and Ease-of-Use instruments for decision making: A confirmatory and multigroup invariance analysis, Decision Sciences, 29(4): 839-869 (1998).
24. Fishbein, M. & Ajzen, I.: Belief, attitude, intention and behavior: An introduction to theory and research. Reading, MA: Addison-Wesley Publishing Company (1975).
25. Hendriks, P.H.J. & Jacobs, W.H.: The lonely comate: The adoption-failure of an intranet-based consumer and market intelligence system. Hershey, PA: Idea Group Publishing, pp. 130-150 (2003).

26. Hu, P.J., Chau, P.Y.K., Liu Sheng, O.R. & Yan Tam, K.: Examining the Technology Acceptance Model using physician acceptance of telemedicine technology, Journal of Management Information Systems, 16(2): 91-112 (1999).
27. Igbaria, M. & Tan, M.: The consequences of information technology acceptance on subsequent individual performance, Information and Management, 32(3): 113-121 (1997).
28. Igbaria, M., Zinatelli, N., Cragg, P. & Cavaye, A.L.M.: Personal Computing acceptance factors in small firms: A Structural Equation Model, MIS Quarterly, 21(3): 279-305 (1997).
29. Ikart, E.M.: Critical success factors for Executive Information Systems usage in organisations, Doctor of Philosophy dissertation, School of Management and Marketing, University of Wollongong, NSW, Australia (2005).
30. Jeyaraj, A., Rottman, J.W. & Lacity, M.C.: A review of the predictors, linkages, and biases in IT innovation and adoption research, Journal of Information Technology, 21: 1-23 (2006).
31. Keil, M., Beranek, P.M. & Konsynski, B.R.: Usefulness and ease of use: Field study evidence regarding task considerations, Decision Support Systems, 13(1): 75-91 (1995).
32. Khalil, O.E. & Elkordy, M.M.: EIS Information: Use and quality determinants, Information Resources Management Journal, 18(2): 68-93 (2005).
33. Lu, H.P. & Gustafson, D.H.: An empirical study of perceived usefulness and perceived ease of use on computerized support system use over time, International Journal of Information Management, 14(5): 317-329 (1994).
34. Miller, J. & Khera, O.: Digital library adoption and the technology acceptance model: A cross-country analysis, The Electronic Journal of Information Systems in Developing Countries, 40(6): 1-19 (2010).
35. Shih, H-P.: Extended technology acceptance model of internet utilization behavior, Information & Management, 41(6): 719-729 (2004).
36. Singh, S., Singh, D.K., Singh, M.K. & Singh, S.K.: The forecasting of 3G market in India based on Revised Technology Acceptance Model, International Journal of Next-Generation Networks (IJNGN), 2(2): 61-68 (2010).
37. Straub, D., Keil, M. & Brenner, W.: Testing technology acceptance model across cultures: A three countries study, Information & Management, 33: 1-11 (1997).
38. Suradi, Z.: Testing Technology Acceptance Model (TAM) in Malaysian environment, BITWorld 2001 Conference Proceedings, American University in Cairo, Egypt, June 4-6 (2001).
39. Vandenbosch, B. & Huff, S.L.: Searching and scanning how executives obtain information from EIS, MIS Quarterly, 21(1): 81-107 (1997).
40. Venkatesh, V.: Creation of favorable user perceptions: Exploring the role of intrinsic motivation, MIS Quarterly, 23(2): 239-260 (1999).
41. Venkatesh, V. & Davis, F.D.: A theoretical extension of the Technology Acceptance Model: Four longitudinal field studies, Management Science, 46(2): 186-204 (2000).

42. Venkatesh, V. & Morris, M.G.: Why don't men ever stop to ask for directions? Gender, social influence, and their role in technology acceptance and usage behavior, MIS Quarterly, 24(1): 115-139 (2000).
43. Venkatesh, V., Morris, M., Davis, G.B. & Davis, F.D.: User acceptance of Information Technology: Toward a unified view, MIS Quarterly, 27(3): 425-478 (2003).
44. Venter, P., van Rensburg, M. & Davis, A.: Drivers of learning management system use in a South African open and distance learning institution, Australasian journal of Educational Technology, 28(2): 183-198 (2012).
45. Walters, B.A., Jiang, J.J. & Klein, G.: Strategic information and strategic decision making: the EIS/CEO interface in smaller manufacturing companies, Information & Management, 40: 487-495 (2003).

www.ingramcontent.com/pod-product-compliance
Lightning Source LLC
Chambersburg PA
CBHW051210050326
40689CB00008B/1256